AN HUMBLE INQUIRY

An Humble Inquiry

into the Scripture-Account of Jesus Christ:

*A Short Argument concerning His
Deity and Glory, according to the Gospel*

by

Thomas Emlyn

UPDATED EDITION

INTRODUCTION BY

Kegan A. Chandler

EDITED BY

Dale Tuggy
Kegan A. Chandler

NASHVILLE

An Humble Inquiry into the Scripture-Account of Jesus Christ: A Short Argument concerning His Deity and Glory, according to the Gospel – Updated Edition

Copyright © 2021 Theophilus Press. All rights reserved. Except for brief quotations in critical publications or reviews, no part of this book may be reproduced in any manner without prior written permission from the publisher.
Write: Information@Theophilus-Press.com

Theophilus Press
P.O. Box 1036
White House, TN 37188

www.theophilus-press.com

Unless otherwise noted, all Bible quotations in the footnotes are from the New Revised Standard Version.

Emlyn, Thomas (1663 – 1741)
Chandler, Kegan A. (1988 – 20xx)
i + 136 pp.

ISBN-13: 978-1-7375783-0-7

Printed in the United States of America

CONTENTS

NOTES ON THIS EDITION — i

INTRODUCTION
"Emlyn's Humble Inquiry: English Unitarianism and
the Rise of Tolerance in the West" by Kegan A. Chandler — 1

An Humble Inquiry — 33

CHAPTER 1: GOD AND JESUS
  1.1 How the Word "God" is Used in Scripture — 35
  1.2 Jesus on Himself as Distinct from and Subordinate to God — 40

CHAPTER 2: THE HUMAN JESUS
  2.1 How Jesus Denies Having Divine Attributes — 51
  2.2 Why "Two-Natures" Speculations Don't Help — 57

CHAPTER 3: ANSWERING OBJECTIONS
  3.1 Answering Scriptural Objections about Christ's Knowledge — 69
  3.2 Answering Arguments from the Worship of Jesus — 90
  3.3 Protestants' Anti-Catholic Arguments Re-applied to Themselves — 97
  3.4 Conclusion: A Call for Temperance — 104

BIBLIOGRAPHY 113

APPENDIX A:
   The Complete Bibliography of Thomas Emlyn 127

SCRIPTURE INDEX 133

NOTES ON THIS EDITION

In this updated edition Emlyn's punctuation has been modernized throughout, deleting many capital letters and italics, and changing references and marginal references to footnotes. Most of the Scripture references are Emlyn's. But as he wrote for a scripturally literate public, he left some out, which we have now added. As was standard, Emlyn used italics instead of quotation marks; these have been changed to quotation marks. The capitalization of the word "god" has been standardized as follows: when it is used as a name or title "God," when it is used as a common noun "god." Words or phrases which have changed meaning or fallen out of use since Emlyn's time have been replaced. Chapter and section headings have also been updated and abbreviated. In so far as we've been able, we have confirmed and updated or corrected his references. Notes reproduced from the 1746 edition of Thomas Emlyn's *Works*, edited by Sollom Emlyn (1697–1754), have been prefaced with "*W.*" All other notes have been supplied by the editors.

INTRODUCTION

Emlyn's Humble Inquiry: English Unitarianism and the Rise of Tolerance in the West

---

"I WROTE MY HUMBLE INQUIRY," said English theologian and preacher Thomas Emlyn, "as one grieved in spirit and afflicted, forsaken by my people and my friends, and abandoned to the accusations, anger, and contempt of all around me, cast out as a despised and broken vessel." While Emlyn was convinced that he had only been "maintaining the cause of the God of gods, and the truth of Jesus his Son," he found himself labeled a "heretic" by his fellow ministers and "numbered among the vilest transgressors and blasphemers."[2] Emlyn's 1702 publication of *An Humble Inquiry*, a spirited defense of unitarian theology, ultimately led to more than the destruction of his reputation. In the eyes of the English government, his opinions about

---

[2] Emlyn, "Narrative," 12, modernized.

INTRODUCTION

God and Jesus were blasphemous and a danger to society. After an unfair trial, Emlyn's wealth was confiscated and he was thrown into prison like a common criminal. In our own time, it may be difficult to imagine how any book of Christian theology, even decidedly "unorthodox" theology, could cause its author so much financial, legal, and bodily suffering. Yet Emlyn's world was one in which the spirit of religious tolerance had only begun to stir.

The last man killed by the state on charges of blasphemy had been the radical Anabaptist Edward Wightman in 1612. Wightman had been executed for his insistence that there is no "Trinity of Persons" in God, that "Jesus Christ is only a man and a mere creature, and not God and man in one person," and that Christ did not exist before his human life.[3] These views were justification enough in the eyes of the English government to burn Wightman at the stake.[4] Modern political activists in the West may often endeavor to rescue

---

[3] Howell, *A Complete Collection*, 735.

[4] Wightman was condemned by King James I, whose letter to the Sherriff of Lichfield described Wightman's theological views as "cursed opinions belched by the instinct of Satan." The king concluded that Wightman must be killed "lest our subjects [be] infect[ed] by his contagion," and "other Christians . . . fall into the same crime." Such executions were thought to be the right of the state, since part of its duty was to "maintain and defend" the catholic faith. In condemning Wightman's views, the king invoked the ancient names "Ebion" (now thought by most to not be an actual person), "Arius," and "Photinus"— ancient unitarian theologians; see King James, "Letter to the Sheriff of Lichfield," quoted in Wallace, *Antitrinitarian Biography*, 567–68.

politics from the encroachment of religion, but after Wightman's death, and in the last quarter of the seventeenth century especially, the intellectual world found itself more squarely focused on the defense of faith, which had long sighed for liberation from government. Indeed, what is the appropriate role of the state, the philosophers openly asked, in enforcing "proper" belief? Does the state's involvement in theology create more problems than it resolves? Is diversity more preservative of social order than forced uniformity? By the middle of the seventeenth century, enough progress was made towards religious tolerance in England that public opposition was able to stifle a 1648 government ordinance which specifically hoped to punish denial of the Trinity with death.[5]

The triumph of the Toleration Act in 1689 signaled freedom for Nonconformists, those Protestants who dissented from both the Roman Catholic Church and the Church of England. It also signaled the failure of the state's dream of a unified Christianity across the kingdom, and revealed how far arguments in the intellectual world had been prodding the nation towards religious tolerance behind the scenes. The arguments of French Calvinist Pierre Bayle in his *Commentaire Philosophique* (1686-88), and those of English philosopher John Locke in his *Letter Concerning Toleration* (1689), had produced especially positive results within the

---

[5] See Makower, *The Constitutional History*, 193, n. 37.

INTRODUCTION

"Republic of Letters," the long-distance network of academics arguing across Europe and the Americas.

While it was clear that a new day was dawning in England, religious intolerance refused to disappear without a fight. As the eighteenth century came into view, it would be Christological debate in particular, with its troubled history and supposed eternal consequences, which would continue to test the nation's resolve towards lenience even a decade after the Toleration Act's passage. This was the anxious scene into which Thomas Emlyn entered and raised his Christological challenge: Jesus was not the one God, Emlyn said, but a human being, a subordinate entity who owed to his sovereign all his teachings and power, even his existence. Emlyn's daring publication of these hazardous opinions in 1702, reprinted with care in the present volume, would severely test the limits of England's religious tolerance.

The conditions of Emlyn's birth seem to foreshadow his eventual showdown with the state. His father, a businessman and Nonconformist-leaning Anglican named Silvester Emlyn, was ousted from his position as regional councilor for his religious views in 1662. One year later, Thomas was born. The boy would go on to receive his education from the Nonconformist George Boheme, and would eventually transfer to Emanuel College, a small academy operated by a dissenting preacher in Northamptonshire. This obscure school, with its modest theological library, proved unable to satisfy young Emlyn's growing curiosity. Hoping to become better connected to modern scholarship, he soon found his way to the theological school of Thomas Doolittle in Islington in 1682. Here he became familiar with not only a wider world of literature and scholarly dialogue, but with Christian ministry, and it was at Doolittle's meeting house that he preached his first sermon on December 19th, 1682.[6]

Emlyn's talents were immediately obvious, as was the independent spirit behind his writing. Less than five months after his preaching began, he was invited to serve as domestic chaplain to the estate of Countess Donegal, a wealthy Presbyterian in Northern Ireland. By 1684, he had moved with the family to Belfast, where he eventually came into the service of Sir William Franklin, whose wealth afforded Emlyn a generous personal allowance. While Emlyn's relationship with Franklin and his household was good and ostensibly one of mutual respect, Emlyn's inquiring mind would soon get in the way of his career. Franklin offered Emlyn an even more comfortable position at his secondary estate in England, if only he would acquiesce to more "orthodox" theological standards by joining the Anglican church. Such an offer proved less attractive to him than theological freedom. He decided instead to accept an invitation to a significant Presbyterian church in Wood Street, Dublin, which received his preaching and writing with enthusiasm. However, Ireland

---

[6] Gibson, "Persecution," 526.

would become increasingly unsafe for Protestants. In 1688, whispers of Catholic uprisings and the impending massacre of Protestants turned to shouts. Memories of earlier Catholic-on-Protestant violence in 1641 gave rise to palpable fear over these rumors, and Emlyn's own congregation grew worried. Emlyn himself began to preach with pistols in his pockets. Ultimately, a variety of occupational factors contributed to Emlyn's desire to leave Ireland for England.

After a brief period of unemployment, in 1689 he accepted a position as the minister of a small English church. During this time, Emlyn began to follow a public controversy between unitarian and trinitarian Christians which had been initiated in 1687 by Stephen Nye's *A Brief History of the Unitarians*, in fact not so much a history as a brief but potent overall case for what was then called a "Socinian" understanding of Christian theology.[7] This was opposed by William Sherlock's *A Vindication of the Doctrine of the Trinity and of the Incarnation of the Son of God*.[8] The controversy swelled into a storm of dozens of pamphlets and books by various sorts of trinitarians and unitarians. Party lines in this controversy were not so neatly drawn, and significant infighting occurred in the trinitarian camp. Sherlock's views were attacked as tritheism and as traitorous to the Church of England by Robert South in his

---

[7] Nye, *A Brief History*.
[8] Sherlock, *A Vindication*.

INTRODUCTION

Animadversions upon Dr. Sherlock's Book entitled a Vindication of the Holy and Ever Blessed Trinity (1693). The fact of this disagreement among trinitarians was emphasized in unitarian arguments.[9] Emlyn and his friend, the Nonconformist minister William Manning (1663-1741), studied Sherlock's book, and another by John Howe,[10] beginning a joint investigation into the Trinity which lasted the duration of their lives.[11] Ultimately, the two researchers were convinced that the doctrine of the Trinity played no part in the preaching of the historical Jesus or the writers of the New Testament. Furthermore, the meaning of the doctrine itself was debatable, and they recognized that even the most respected trinitarian scholars of their day could not settle on

---

[9] "One would expect that since they say that the Trinity is the doctrine of the catholic or universal Church, and necessary to be believed in order to be saved, that at least they know and were agreed what this Trinity is, or what is thereby meant, else we are required to believe nobody knows what in order to be saved. But so it is; there is as much confusion, in declaring what this catholic, necessary doctrine is, as there was at the building of Babel, when no one understood one another . . . they have nothing left in which they agree but only the word 'Trinity.' " Nye, *Observations*, 8, modernized.

[10] Howe, *A Calm*.

[11] Much of this investigation was carried out in letters between the two. Segments of this correspondence, which largely took place between 1703 and 1710, were preserved by Manning's great-grandson, also named William Manning (d. 1825). These portions were reproduced in several editions of the English unitarian periodical owned by the British and Foreign Unitarian Association, *Monthly Repository* (1817, 1825, 1826). The originals have been lost.

INTRODUCTION

an interpretation which satisfactorily preserved monotheism. Later, Emlyn would write of this revelation:

> I admit that I had been unsettled in my notions from the time I read Dr. Sherlock's book on the Trinity, which sufficiently revealed how far many were gone back toward polytheism. I long tried what I could do with some Sabellian turns, making out a Trinity of somewhats in one single mind.[12] I found that by the tritheistical scheme of Dr. Sherlock and Mr. Howe, I best preserved a Trinity, but I lost the Unity. By the Sabellian scheme of modes, and subsistences, and properties, etc., I best kept up the divine Unity, but then I had lost a Trinity such as the Scripture reveals, so that I could never keep both in view at once. But after much serious thought and study of the Holy Scriptures, with many serious prayers to the Father of lights, I found great reason first to doubt, and after, by degrees, to alter my judgment in relation to formerly received opinions of the Trinity, and the supreme deity of our Lord Jesus Christ.[13]

---

[12] That there are "three somewhats" in God was the proposal of John Wallis (*The Doctrine*). Wallis suggested that if the word "person" is undesirable, then it could be said that "In God there are three names or titles, three capacities or respects, three relations, three considerations, three notions, three modes." Wallis, quoted in Nye, *Observations,* 10. Unitarian writers countered that such an ambiguous proposition represented only a verbal difference from their views: "Now how can he, who believes in such a Trinity of Somewhats or Persons as this, write against the Socinians? They believe the Trinity as much as Dr. Wallis." Nye, *Observations,* 10. For the controversy between Wallis, Sherlock, South, and the unitarians, see Trowell, "Unitarian and/or Anglican," 85–93, and Dixon, *Nice and Hot.*

[13] Emlyn, "Narrative," 15–16, modernized.

INTRODUCTION

Manning eventually became persuaded of the "Socinian" Christology—that Jesus was a man distinct from God who began to exist in the womb of Mary—and he worked earnestly to show Emlyn its truth.[14] But Emlyn, while adopting a unitarian theology, could not release himself from the personal pre-existence of the Son, and argued for this subordinationist view in many amicable letters with Manning.[15] While some later reports describe Emlyn as having eventually come to the "Socinian" view, his son and

---

[14] This Christology, which rejected the pre-existence of Christ yet maintained the virgin birth, was so named after the Italian theologians of the Minor Reformed Church in Poland, Lelio Sozzini (1525–62) and Fausto Sozzini (1539–1604). The "Socinians" were not the first, however, to hold to such a view, which can be found among such ancient figures as Photinus (d. 376 CE), Artemon (c. 240 CE), Theodotus of Byzantium (c. 190 CE), and the Jewish "Nazarenes" of the first century CE; see Gaston, *Dynamic Monarchianism* (2021). Such views are currently represented by the modern theological movement known as "biblical unitarianism"; see Hyndman, "Biblical Monotheism Today."

[15] "Subordinationist" is perhaps the best way to describe Emlyn's unitarian views, in which a pre-existent Son was both derived from, subject to, and ontologically lesser than the one God. While many have approached Emlyn with the "Arian" label, still so often used to describe subordinationist theologies which include a pre-existent Son, this was a term Emlyn would have rejected, since he saw himself in full agreement with neither the historical "Arians" nor with Arius himself; see Emlyn, "Narrative," 16. Emlyn preferred instead to call himself simply a "unitarian" Christian.

INTRODUCTION

biographer, recounting his father's legacy in his memoirs, reports that this was not the case.[16]

Having arrived at unitarian views, Emlyn knew very well the disdain his new theology and Christology would earn him, even among his fellow Dissenters. Despite recent progress towards religious liberty, his future remained a road as dangerous as it was uncharted. Nevertheless, he trusted that his recent inquiries, however much contempt they might earn him, would ultimately fare well in God's eyes:

> There is nothing I more sincerely desire than right knowledge of important truths; I am sure I am not biased by interest or love for worldly esteem; and if one should err unwillingly about the blessed Jesus, I should hope it may be pardoned, though it would sincerely grieve me to promote any such thing. I think the clouds and darkness that surround us and others make this world an undesirable stage of confusion. May I know God and Christ so as to love them and be transformed into a divine likeness! And then surely the wished-for day will come, when that which is imperfect shall be done away.[17]

In May of 1691, Emlyn returned to Dublin, having accepted an offer to co-pastor a large Presbyterian church with his friend Joseph Boyse. In 1694, he married Esther Bury, whose finances allowed them a comfortable life. But Emlyn's

---

[16] See "Memoirs," xiv.
[17] Thomas Emlyn, "Letter to William Manning, January 18th, 1697," in "Memoirs," xix–xx, modernized.

thoughts on the Trinity threatened to shatter this peace. In 1697 he wrote to Manning about his expectation that if he ever made his disavowal of the Trinity known to his congregation or the Presbyterian leadership in Dublin, he would immediately lose his preaching post. Emlyn waited in this quiet posture for several years, prepared to speak his mind if anyone asked.

In 1701, Emlyn's life took a tragic turn. First came the loss of a young and beloved son. Then, suddenly, came the death of his wife Esther. Weeks later, his mother was also dead. Emlyn described these serial losses as "enough to teach me the vanity of all present things, and to draw my thoughts and desires into that world, whither they are translated."[18] Less than six months later, Emlyn's sorrows only increased as he revealed his views on the Trinity.

A member of Emlyn's church, a physician named Duncan Cummins, began to notice his pastor's avoidance of certain common phrases and references to the Trinity in his sermons. Wary of his orthodoxy, he called on Emlyn to cure his suspicions in the presence of his co-minister Joseph Boyse. Now at the moment of truth, Emlyn admitted his views, confessing God the Father as the only Supreme Being and the Son as derived from God. The resulting shock gave way to a meeting of the deacons, which in turn led to a hearing of a Dublin ministers association. The conference was stunned by

---

[18] Emlyn, "Memoirs," xxii.

INTRODUCTION

the non-trinitarian convictions of a man so widely esteemed as Emlyn. When Emlyn offered his resignation to the elders of his own church, they suggested he leave for London and await their decision. The association forbade him to preach anywhere while in England, and Emlyn agreed not to speak about the Trinity but insisted that they could not forbid him to preach at all. In Emlyn's absence, the association did what they could to stir up public resentment, and denounced him from the pulpit as a heretic and blasphemer. In September of 1702, Boyse wrote to him from Dublin about the ministers' opposition:

> they look upon your opinion itself as a dangerous error, and are unwilling that any flame of contention about it should break out here. And indeed the prejudices of most run so high, that unless you could entirely embrace the common faith and even use the common language, your post here would be uneasy, were you readmitted to it. [19]

Boyse himself could not be persuaded of Emlyn's opinions, hating the whole discussion and calling disputes over the Trinity an "unhappy controversy, which above all others I wish were buried in silence, as foreseeing no good to the interest of Christianity by the revival of it."[20] While Boyse concluded that Emlyn was, despite his views, a genuine seeker

---

[19] Joseph Boyse, "Letter to Thomas Emlyn from Dublin, September 3, 1702," quoted in Matthews, *An Account,* 19–20.
[20] Quoted in Drummond, *An Explanation*, 47.

of truth, the other ministers continued to see him as a dangerous troublemaker.[21]

Exiled and feeling desperate in London, Emlyn sought to confer with sympathetic Christians.[22] One of these must have been the notorious, learned, and prolific Anglican priest Stephen Nye, initiator of the aforementioned controversy, who Emlyn surely knew about from his reading. In the early 1690s, Nye followed up his 1687 book with a series of carefully argued yet sharp-elbowed anonymous unitarian tracts, in which he categorized, refuted, and ridiculed various Trinity theories.[23]

But starting in 1695, Nye veered in the direction of orthodoxy.[24] He argued that believers in a "real" Trinity think there are three divine minds or beings or individuals, which is heretical tritheism. In contrast, believers in a "nominal" Trinity hold that in the one divine being, God, there are three divine actions or properties, which is all God's being "three Persons" amounts to, which is something, Nye thought, unitarians should agree with. Thus, he argued that the orthodox position is the same as the unitarian one: God as a single self ("person," in the sense of an intelligent being); the

---

[21] Boyse would eventually mount his own theological defense against Emlyn in 1704, responding directly to his *Inquiry*. See Boyse, *True Deity*, i–ii.

[22] "Narrative," 22–23.

[23] For a summary and sources see Dixon, *Nice and Hot*, chapters 4–5.

[24] This is seen in a series of his publications starting with his *A Discourse*.

disagreement between unitarians and "nominal" trinitarians is only verbal. Perhaps trinitarians' language is needlessly confusing, but the "nominal" position is correct.

In following publications, Nye's position became increasingly catholic and sympathetic to traditional trinitarian language and speculations. By 1701, he was ready to publicly defend his understanding of the Trinity, this time in his own name rather than anonymously as before.[25] It seems that, unlike many unitarian Christians, Nye's only reason for being a unitarian was to preserve monotheism, and when he came to think that he could do this through what has more recently been called a "one-self" Trinity theory, he declared himself orthodox and trinitarian. But unlike many trinitarians of his time, Nye believed in full religious freedom.

In 1702, less than three months after leaving Ireland, Emyln published his first short public response to the accusing Dublin ministers.[26] A reader familiar with Nye's voluminous output can discern his theological fingerprints all over this text; one infers that Emlyn discussed his plight with Nye, and that Nye suggested a conciliating, short reply.[27] Perhaps Nye

---

[25] Nye, *The Doctrine*; Nye, *Resolution*; Nye, *Institutions*. On how his *Resolution* relates to Emlyn, see note 27 below.

[26] Emlyn, *The Case*.

[27] Nye continued to take an interest in the Emlyn controversy. In 1703 in London, Emlyn's *An Humble Inquiry* was reprinted as part 1 of *Two Treatises*, with part 2 being *A Resolution of the Objections against the Doctrine of the Holy Trinity: together with the Church-Terms of Communion relating to that Doctrine*, which was anonymous but

INTRODUCTION

even helped him to write it. Here, Emlyn all too briefly suggests, implausibly, that he and his accusers really agree in substance, if not in words, about the Trinity and the Incarnation. But this requires the Nye-ish construal of the Trinity as a single self in which there are "three modal distinctions," it being suggested that the "Persons" of God amount to his being "Creator, Redeemer, and Sanctifier."[28] Echoing Nye, Emlyn writes that God "may be as much three as man's soul is, in which is understanding, will, and life, all in one single spirit."[29] And the catholic "Incarnation" doctrine is likewise Nye-ishly construed as "That this infinite God is in an unspeakable manner united to and present with the man Christ Jesus."[30] Can't his accusers agree with him about these things, Emlyn insists, leaving fine philosophical distinctions and theories aside?[31] Least plausibly, he suggests that their

---

obviously authored by Nye. Here, Nye is trying to exploit the Emyln controversy to promote his theological "solution" as propounded in his *The Doctrine* and his *Institutions*. Again, Nye seems to have been the author of an anonymous tract which argues directly to the jury that had recently convicted Emlyn that his views are not blasphemous and should be legally tolerated, especially since in some respects they resemble the views of learned and respected Anglican bishops. (Nye, *A Sober Expostulation*.)

[28] Emlyn, *The Case*, 45. Compare: Nye, *A Resolution*, 22; Nye, *A Discourse*, 8, 18; Nye, *Institutions*, 183–84.

[29] Emlyn, *The Case*, 45. Compare: Nye, *Institutions*, 182.

[30] Nye, *Institutions*, 182. Compare: Nye, *A Discourse*, 18, 40; Nye, *The Doctrine*, 42; Nye, *Resolution*, 14, 19.

[31] Emlyn, *The Case*, 46.

disagreement about worship is basically verbal: what they call "Christ" he calls "God," and they agree that he alone should be worshiped. Of course, Emlyn adds that "Christ" properly refers to the man Jesus, although he can be called "God."[32] And while Christ can be described as having divine attributes, Emlyn opines that these should be understood as having to do with the God who is working through him, or else "if taken in a qualified sense, they may be understood properly of the exalted man Christ."[33] Finally, Emlyn urges that he never meant to cause controversy, that his hand was forced by "an importunate and repeated demand," and that his whole aim has been just to know the revealed truth of the gospel.[34]

This too-short, defensive, conciliating reply only made things worse for Emlyn. The Dublin ministers had no sympathy for his minimalist, Nye-ish takes on the Trinity and the Incarnation, and issued a blistering reply, which was composed on their behalf by Emlyn's former colleague Joseph Boyse.[35] They accused him, reasonably, of hiding his real views, which they knew from their conversations with him in Dublin. He'd admitted that Jesus can be called "God," but they pointed out that in earlier conversations, he'd said that Jesus was called "God" "only by office and deputation" rather

---

[32] *The Case*, 47–48. On Jesus being called "God" see chapter 1 below.
[33] *The Case*, 48.
[34] *The Case*, 49.
[35] Boyse, *The Difference*.

INTRODUCTION

than "by nature and essence."³⁶ Rejecting Emlyn's suggestion of understanding the Trinity along the lines of Nye's "nominal trinitarians," they asserted that the Persons of the Trinity are all equally God, and that this Trinity represents three objects of worship, not one.³⁷ Moreover, the Incarnation is not merely that God indwells and operates through the man Jesus. Rather, Christ has both a divine and a human nature, and must be worshiped as God, for Scripture (they think) teaches that "divine worship should be given to none to whom the perfections and rights of the divine nature do not belong."³⁸ They characterize Emlyn's position as "Arian," suggest that Scripture only distinguishes Jesus from God "as man," and insist that the divine attribute of omniscience is clearly ascribed to Christ in Scripture.³⁹

The problem was that Emlyn had tried to keep the peace but had said little about his own opinions and why he had come to hold them. Evidently, Emlyn realized that he should explain his actual views on what the Bible teaches about God and Jesus. Thus, when he returned to Dublin to settle his affairs and arrange for a permanent move to England, Emlyn began writing the book you now hold, a testimony to his long

---

[36] *The Difference*, 8.
[37] *The Difference*, 2. Nye had insisted that rightly understood the Trinity amounts to only one object or recipient of worship. See Nye, *A Discourse*, 32.
[38] *The Difference*, 3–5.
[39] *The Difference*, 7–11.

study of the Scriptures regarding God and his human Son. In 1702, Emlyn's *An Humble Inquiry* was born.

In this tract Emlyn approaches the question of Christ's identity by considering how frequently and how thoroughly the New Testament writers distinguish God and Jesus. The Father and Son are, in his words, "two disparates, or different things," and the New Testament clearly and constantly testifies to that truth: Jesus was, and is, the "image of God"—and if anyone is an image of anything, by definition he cannot be that thing. And the Gospel preaching of Jesus himself, he argues, quite clearly demonstrates the man's submission and obedience to God the Father. Jesus had emphasized his lack of underived power, absolute goodness, and unlimited knowledge. Emlyn concludes that recourse to dual-natures speculations is of little use here and only muddies the waters. The unitarian interpretation, on which God is one being and Jesus is another, is a much better solution, and despite popular arguments could be easily maintained, even in light of the few biblical texts which appear to name Christ "God." Such figures as Moses and the angels, he points out, had already been referred to as "gods" in Scripture. In a similar way, Emlyn refutes popular arguments for Christ's deity on the basis of his miracles—again, other biblical figures like the apostles had healed diseases and raised the dead. For Emlyn, Jesus is the great messenger, mediator, prophet, Messiah, and judge of the whole world—he is absolutely everything which the

Scriptures declare him to be, and this is all due to the will and power of the one God whom he had faithfully served, not to some additional, divine nature within him. The deity of Christ and the Trinity were ultimately not necessary for explaining the biblical data, and only harm Christian theology.

Emlyn dexterously employs the opinions of other scholars in his case: Anglican voices like Archbishop Tillotson and Daniel Whitby had both already admitted that Scripture nowhere asserts Jesus' ontological equality with the Father. This silence demonstrated that belief in the deity of Christ is unnecessary for Christians. Furthermore, such doctrines only hindered the progress of the faith. Citing secular historians, Emlyn points out that missionary efforts in China had been thwarted by the difficult concept of a mortal God. Scholar Meric Casaubon, he also notes, had acknowledged that the doctrine of the Incarnation was more alienating than any other doctrine and that it has unfortunately kept many people from embracing the Christian religion. This fact, Emlyn argues, and which Casaubon claimed he could demonstrate from history, should at the very least give Christians pause about the dogma's value.[40]

Emlyn also considers the Apostles' Creed, and cites both its early origins and its startling lack of any reference to the deity of Christ or the Trinity. Also important are the opinions

---

[40] See below, pp. 109-110.

of the earliest church fathers, who agree explicitly with his subordination of the Son to the Father, and also the notice of Justin Martyr that there existed Christians in his day (mid-second century CE) who denied the pre-existence (and thus the deity) of Jesus.[41]

Noteworthy also is Emlyn's insistence that his Protestant opponents, who had charged him with innovation in light of a perceived lack of traditional precedent, have frustrated their own historical arguments against their Roman Catholic adversaries. In the face of Catholic charges that their traditions did not exist before Luther, these Protestants had argued that their theological principles were able to be found in the Scriptures, and that their church, so to speak, was present in the earliest Christians. These same Protestants had now challenged unitarians like Emlyn to show them what historical Christian church believed that Christ was not God, and had rejected unitarian arguments that theirs is the original and biblical faith. And many such Protestant defenses against Catholicism, Emlyn argues, are spoiled by their haphazard attempts to deal with unitarianism. Standing squarely upon "Protestant standards," he writes that "unitarians think they can stand their ground and defend themselves in these matters as easily as the Protestants can against the Catholics."[42]

---

[41] See below, pp. 104-6.
[42] See below, p. 101.

INTRODUCTION

Emlyn also exploits the trinitarian controversies of his day, highlighting the evident discord among Christian leaders regarding the proper interpretation of the Trinity. Two parties exist, he explains, the first of which hold there to be three real persons or intelligent beings in God, and the other, only one. This represents what has been called three-self and one-self interpretations of the Trinity among modern scholars.[43] Emlyn sees both of these approaches as impossible to reconcile with monotheism and the biblical data about Jesus' relationships to God and to us: three equally divine selves, despite popular arguments to the contrary, would be three gods, while reducing Jesus and the Spirit to modes or properties of one divine being dissolves Christ's role as mediator. Thus the unitarian option, completely separating the God of the Bible and his Messiah, is the only way to preserve and honor the apostolic tradition about the two, a tradition which Emlyn feels is not lurking somewhere within

---

[43] For a modern defense of the monotheism of three-self views, popularly known as social trinitarianism, see Hasker, "Objections to Social Trinitarianism." Regarding one-self trinitarianism, "Influential 20th century theologians Karl Barth (1886–1968) and Karl Rahner (1904–84) endorse one-self Trinity theories, and suggest alternative terms for 'person' for what the triune God is three of. They argue that 'person' has come in modern times to mean a self. But three divine selves would be three gods. Hence, even if 'person' should be retained as traditional, its meaning in the context of the Trinity should be expounded using phrases like 'modes of being' (Barth) or 'manners of subsisting' (Rahner)" (Tuggy, "Trinity"). For a modern case for a one-self Trinity see Leftow, "Anti-Social Trinitarianism."

the text and waiting for the sprightly hands of later scholars to tease it out—no, the apostles' tradition about God and Jesus, that is, their true distinction between these two beings, is clear and bold on every page. One need only consult the early church's own written account of their origins and their most original views: when the apostles baptized thousands in the book of Acts, says Emlyn, they did so without informing them that Christ was Almighty God. "How can this be," he writes, "if the supreme deity of Christ is a fundamental teaching of the Christian faith? Likewise, [Peter] later preaches that 'God was with him.' This was all."[44] Indeed, in Emlyn's view, no solution from the orthodox camps, which all claim to safeguard the oldest and most true version of trinitarianism, could match the clarity and simplicity of the unitarian approach.

Emlyn's *Inquiry* is a succinct, erudite, and carefully reasoned case. But despite his intentions, its immediate effect was only greater persecution. Emlyn's biographers have called it a blessing that his recently deceased family members had been spared the misery which began to afflict him six months after their deaths. The book's printing significantly worsened the conflict in Dublin, and more quickly than Emlyn had imagined. Indeed, he had originally planned to leave

---

[44] See below, p. 97.

permanently for London several days after its printing, but these plans were dramatically interrupted.

While it had been printed anonymously, those familiar with the controversy knew the author immediately. Two members of his former church, a Baptist and a Presbyterian, took the writing to the Dublin Grand Jury. They petitioned the Lord Chief Justice of Ireland for a special warrant, which they received, on the basis of public blasphemy laws. Emlyn was promptly arrested and taken to jail. His bail was set at a stunning eight-hundred pounds—a serious amount marking a serious crime. However, this charge of blasphemy seems to have previously been applied to only scornful, derisive, and anti-Christian remarks, and the only precedent offered by the Lord Chief Justice was a case in which Jesus had been aggressively denounced as a "bastard and a whoremaster."[45] This was supposed, rather absurdly, to resemble Emlyn's case.

After a bout of procedural and clerical delays, Emlyn finally took the stand in June of 1703. He was charged with having written and printed a book of impious opinion. He would not be allowed to give his own defense, he was told, but that he would instead simply be "run down like a wolf without law or game."[46] Emlyn had trouble acquiring

---

[45] That is, "a whoremonger." Such was the crime of a Mr. Taylor, who said, "Jesus Christ is a bastard and a whoremaster, religion is a cheat, and I fear neither God, the devil, nor man," cited in Emlyn, "Narrative," 12.

[46] Attributed to Sir Richard Levins, later chief justice of the Court of Common Pleas; cited in Wallace, *Antitrinitarian Biography*, 517.

counsel, but finally did, in the form of one Mr. Broderick. Nevertheless, the trial—if it can be called that—proceeded so swiftly and with such unfairness that the intimidated jury had no choice but to deliver the verdict which the Chief Justice so obviously desired.[47] Emlyn's sentence was a year's imprisonment and a staggering fine of one thousand pounds. One member of the jury, feeling terrible about his own role in this conviction, would later apologize to Emlyn.[48]

In hope of reducing his fine and sentence, it was suggested that Emlyn should write a letter to the Lord Chief Justice from his prison cell. It read, in part:

> I have no greater desire than to learn the truth from the Holy Scriptures. If I am mistaken in my opinions, God knows, it is altogether unwillingly. It is most obvious that I have forfeited my interest, and sacrificed my reputation in the world, and exposed myself to such evils, as nothing could ever make me submit to, but the real fear of offending God; which your Lordship will, I doubt not, admit is a very great reason. I am ready to do anything consistent with my judgment and conscience; but I am afraid to do that, for fear of shame from men, for which, my conscience may suggest to me, that Jesus Christ will be ashamed of me at the great day.[49]

---

[47] See Gibbon, "Persecution," 530.
[48] Emlyn, "Narrative," 30–32.
[49] Thomas Emlyn, cited in Wallace, *Antitrinitarian Biography*, 521.

INTRODUCTION

The plea fell on deaf ears. The Chief Justice said that if the trial had been conducted in Spain or Portugal, he would have been immediately burned at the stake—such was the degree of England's progress towards tolerance.[50] Nevertheless, the English authorities did what they could to him. They pinned damnatory papers to his chest and paraded him around the court houses, subjecting him to the scorn of the community. The court told him that it should put him in chains and lock his neck and hands in the pillory, but because he was an educated man they would generously spare him this particular grief.

After his public shaming was finished, he was left to contemplate his sins in his cell. Surrounded by a host of incarcerated debtors, Emlyn did not cease his preaching while in prison. And all the while he never did, at least not in writing, hesitate on his difficult course. As he would famously write:

> I thank God that He did not call me to this lot of suffering till I had arrived at maturity of judgment and firmness of resolution, and that He did not desert me when my friends did. He never let me be so cast down as to renounce the truth or to waver in my faith.[51]

During his internment, his friend, antagonist, and former co-minister Mr. Boyse wrote letters frequently on Emlyn's

---

[50] Wilbur, *A History of Unitarianism*, 245.
[51] Thomas Emlyn, quoted in Mott, "Growth of Unitarian Thought," 301.

behalf, pleading to have his financial penalty reduced. Other distinguished persons, including the Duke of Ormond, the lawyer Thomas Edlicote, and the Lord Chancellor Sir Richard Cox, also intervened to reduce his inhumane treatment and the severity of his fine. Emlyn's imprisonment also stirred up concern among the educated; his prosecution was criticized in Bishop Benjamin Hoadly's "Dedication to Pope Clement XI," published pseudonymously in 1715.[52] In light of all this, the government finally relented, leaving Emlyn with a balance of seventy pounds. He would be forced to pay an additional twenty by the time all was done. The imprisonment had lasted more than two years, from June 1703 to July 1705.

Upon his release, Emlyn resumed his plan to leave Ireland for London and to continue his public preaching there. But this too was a plan interrupted. As soon as he began teaching in London, working without pay for a small congregation at Cutler's Hall, a famous writer named Charles Leslie condemned him in print,[53] and several other newspapers joined in. After formal complaints were lodged with London

---

[52] This was a satirical dedication to Pope Clement XI, published under the pseudonym "Richard Steele," and attached to his *Account of the State of the Roman Catholic Religion Throughout the World* (1715). About Emlyn, the text read, in part: "The Non-conformists accused him, the Conformists condemned him, the Secular power was called in, and the cause ended in an imprisonment and a very great fine: two methods of conviction about which the gospel is silent" (Steele, *Account,* xlviii).

[53] See Leslie, *The Rehearsal.*

authorities, and after a short defense, Emlyn finally gave up his humble preaching post and retired from public view.

As Emlyn's renown as "one who had suffered more than any other man of his time for freedom of conscience" continued to grow,[54] controversy over the Trinity raged on in England. Emlyn became friends with the unitarian scholar William Whiston (1667–1752), successor to Isaac Newton at Cambridge.[55] Some have credited Emlyn's work as a direct influence on the arguments of famed apologist, philosopher, and theologian Samuel Clarke (1675–1729), and it is easy to see why.[56] Though the two would not meet until a decade after *An Humble Inquiry's* publication, Clarke's landmark *Scripture Doctrine of the Trinity* (1712) would share much in common with Emlyn's biblical and philosophical concerns.[57]

---

[54] Wilbur, *A History of Unitarianism*, 246.

[55] Whiston quit the Church of England for the Baptists around 1747 after rejecting the Athanasian Creed. He founded a group of scholars intent on resuscitating what he called "primitive Christianity," which met at his home from 1715–17. Thomas Emlyn was among those invited to participate. Whiston mentions Emlyn's work and his debate with Mr. Boyse in his own account of the pagan origins of the Trinity; see Whiston, *True Origin*, 107.

[56] In Emlyn's *Remarks on Mr. Charles Leslie's First Dialogue* initially published anonymously, Emlyn refers to himself as "a true scriptural trinitarian," anticipating Clarke's similar approach to describing his own subordinationist views in his *Scripture-Doctrine*.

[57] Clarke's publication was divided into three parts. The first section featured all of the New Testament texts about the Father, Son, and Spirit, sorted by what they assert, including several hundred passages in which the Father is presented as the only or most supreme God. In the second

Clarke and Emlyn would become friends, as well as co-conspirators of sorts, working quietly to remove the need for certain theological commitments in order to hold public and preaching posts in England.[58] Several other public controversies over the Trinity, and the need for churches to subscribe to it, would erupt in England, each of which traceable in some way back to Emlyn's *Inquiry*.[59] As one historian of the period has observed, Emlyn's subordinationist views became the prevailing heresy of the early eighteenth century.[60]

In 1719 Emlyn was still considered too controversial to be to be allowed to preach publicly.[61] In 1722, English newspapers continued to label him a chief enemy of orthodox

---

section, he set out his own subordinationist unitarian doctrine, and in the last, he suggested revisions to the liturgy of the Church of England. For Clark, it is clear that the one God is not the Trinity, though he would have been opposed to the "unitarian" and "anti-trinitarian" labels. For him, "unitarian," meant "Socinian," and Clarke disagreed with these about the pre-existence of Christ and other matters. While many have wanted to tag him with the label, he explicitly rejected being called an "Arian" (see Colligan, *The Arian Movement*, 37), as did his friend Emlyn. For a recent discussion of Clarke's doctrine, see Pfizenmaier, *Trinitarian Theology*.

[58] Gibson, "Persecution," 536.

[59] See, for example, the Salter's Hall controversy at Exeter in 1719. Here, at a conference of Dissenting ministers, a slim majority voted for freedom in regard to the doctrine of the Trinity; see Thomas, "The Salters' Hall Debate," 162–86; see also Gibson, "Persecution," 536.

[60] Michael R. Watts, cited in Van Den Berg, *Religious Currents*, 184, n. 10.

[61] Gibson, "Persecution," 536–37.

Christianity.⁶² The American colonies, which had emerged already as a haven for independent thought, were introduced to Emlyn's *Inquiry* in 1756. The work made its debut among a circle of ministers in Boston who were convinced of its truth. And by 1760, Emlyn's book had caused quite a stir, and was selling rapidly. By the time of his American success, however, Emlyn had already died in 1741 at the age of seventy-eight. He was buried in Bunhill Fields in London, with a memorial to his persecution.⁶³

By 1747 it was clear that Emlyn had become a hero for dissenting Christians in England.⁶⁴ His popularity as an emblem of the need for religious tolerance rose to similar heights in America. Extracts from his *Inquiry* were later republished in Boston in 1790, and the text continued to earn scholarly attention, including criticism from Aaron Burr, later Vice President of the United States (1801–05) and at the time a Presbyterian minister and second president of the College of New Jersey (later Princeton University).⁶⁵ Indeed, Emlyn's

---

⁶² See Mist, *A Collection of Miscellany Letters*, 97; Gibson, "Persecution," 537.

⁶³ His inscription says that he was, "to the shame and reproach of a Christian country, persecuted even to bonds and imprisonment, and the spoiling [i.e. confiscation] of his goods, for having maintained the supreme unequalled majesty of the one God and Father of all"; cited in Gibson, "Persecution," 538.

⁶⁴ See Gibson, "Persecution," 537.

⁶⁵ The 1790 American edition, *Extracts from an Humble Inquiry,* was significantly abridged, and was rebutted the next year by Caleb Alexander in his *Real Deity.*

Inquiry continued to provoke responses in both England and America long after his death, and it might be said that only his legacy as an icon of religious freedom outpaced the memory of his arguments. In 1823, the president of Harvard wrote that "among the victims of religious persecution, few have been more conspicuous, or suffered with a purer or nobler mind" than Emlyn.[66] But even this legacy, and the attendant legacy of orthodox persecution of non-trinitarians England, is one which has faded from recent memory.

William Gibson has argued that Emlyn's persecution teaches us several lessons. First, despite the Toleration Act's passage, the impulse of both the Church of England and the state in Emlyn's time was still to punish the "unorthodox"; second, such persecution was not limited to the Church of England, but included other Protestants as well; and third, Emlyn's persecution, due to the attention it gained, brought his unitarian theological views into mainstream discussion.[67] But there is more to Emlyn's legacy.

---

[66] Sparks, *A Collection*, 175. Sparks, a unitarian minister and president of Harvard College (now Harvard University) published some of Emlyn's works in Boston in 1823, and here he described Emlyn's *Inquiry* as "a fair specimen of Mister Emlyn's mode of thinking, his powers of reasoning, and style of composition. To explain and convince is in every part the obvious purpose of the author, and his main effort is to come to the argument with the fewest words, and by the shortest course. A clearer exposition of his opinions, and a more natural and connected chain of reasoning to support them, could not well be imagined" (Sparks, *A Collection*, 206).

[67] See Gibson, "Persecution," 537.

INTRODUCTION

In a similar way that the writings of John Locke have had an unseen influence on Western culture—indeed, without his work, our modern notions of civil, natural, and property rights, and the role of the government in protecting those rights, might not exist—Emlyn has likewise had an unseen effect on our notions of religious tolerance. Without Emlyn's persecution, we wonder if the theological freedom promised by the Toleration Act of 1689 would ever have been realized. Emlyn might have cowered in submission, he might have renounced his *Inquiry* and gone back to a quiet life and never tested the freedom which England promised but proved reluctant to give. In this way Emlyn reveals his value as perhaps the key subject in England's first official experiment with religious liberty. While John Locke's *Letter Concerning Toleration* (1689) is now called "the most eloquent plea for religious toleration,"[68] Emlyn's persecution must be called something similar, though his plea for religious tolerance was one lived out not only on paper, but also before a hostile judge and an angry mob. We learn also from this story the value of unitarian theology in the history of religious freedom. Indeed, challenges to the doctrine of the Trinity, as we have seen, formed the epicenter of the struggle for religious freedom in England in the eighteenth century.

---

[68] Van Doren, *The Joy of Reading*, 220. For a modern edition, see Locke, "A Letter."

INTRODUCTION

Emlyn's *Inquiry*, now more than three hundred years old, still contains as much power to inspire as it did when it was first composed—though whether one will be inspired to agreement or not may depend very much on the assumptions one starts with. Emlyn's most basic desire was to see all manner of Christians moved to ask important questions about tradition—especially the risky sort of questions which widen the eyes of our most beloved preachers and scholars. Few questions, in Emlyn's eyes, seemed more urgent than the identity of the Christian God, and for him, chasing this truth was not only the most genuine way to live but a crucial step in following Christ. To love the God that Jesus loved, that is, the Father, was next. Regardless of one's theological persuasion, it will be hard to ignore Emlyn's love, sincerity, and the humility with which he inquired.

— Kegan A. Chandler

An Humble INQUIRY INTO THE SCRIPTURE-ACCOUNT OF JESUS CHRIST:

OR, A SHORT ARGUMENT Concerning His Deity and Glory, According to the GOSPEL.

---

1 Cor. viii. 5. *To us there is but One God, and he is the Father, of whom are all things; and One Lord, viz. Jesus Christ, through whom are all things.*

Auguſ. cont. Maxim. l. 3. c. 14.
Nec ego *Nicanam* Synodum tibi, nec tu *Ariminenſem* mihi debes, objicere. Scripturarum Authoritatibus, &c.
Thou shalt not urge me with the Council of Ariminum, *nor I thee with the Council of* Nice, *but let us decide the Cauſe by Scripture Authority*

Printed in the Year MDCCII.

To us there is but one God, namely the Father, of whom are all things; and one Lord, namely Jesus Christ, through whom are all things.

1 Corinthians 8:6

You shall not try to persuade me with the Council of Ariminum, nor I you with the Council of Nicaea; but let us decide the question by Scripture authority.[1]

Augustine, *Answer to Maximinus the Arian*, 2.14.3

---

[1] In a recent translation the full passage is: "I should not, however, introduce the Council of Nicaea to prejudice the case in my favor, nor should you introduce the Council of Ariminum that way. I am not bound by the authority of Ariminum, and you are not bound by that of Nicaea. By the authority of the scriptures that are not the property of anyone, but the common witnesses for both of us, let position do battle with position, case with case, reason with reason." Augustine, *Answer to Maximinus*, 282 (2.14.3). Augustine is referring to the councils of catholic bishops at Nicaea in 325 and at Ariminum in 359. On these councils see Hanson, *The Search*, chapters 6, 12.

CHAPTER 1: God and Jesus

1.1 *How the Word "God" is Used in Scripture*

THAT THE BLESSED JESUS HAS THE TITLE of "God" ascribed sometimes to him in the holy Scriptures is not denied by Arians or Socinians.[2] But it remains to be examined in what sense that title as given to him is intended. Nor is this an unreasonable or needless inquiry,

---

[2] Emyln here employs somewhat standard if misleading names for two types of belief among unitarian Christians. (Compare: Irons et. al., *The Son of God*.) Both hold that the one true God is the Father alone, while the "Arians" believe and the "Socinians" deny that Jesus existed before his human life. "Arians" are so called because of the broad similarity of their views to the so-called "Arians" of the fourth century (catholic Christians who opposed the Nicene creed), and "Socinians" are so-called because of unitarian reformer Fausto Paolo Sozzini (a.k.a. Faustus Socinus, 1539–1604), on whose Christology the man Jesus began to exist at the time of his miraculous conception. The labels mislead because most who currently hold such views are not at all followers of either ancient "Arians" or of Socinus; rather, their views are based on their understanding of Scripture.

CHAPTER 1: GOD AND JESUS

since it is beyond all reasonable denial that the title of "God" is given in very different senses in the Scripture.

Sometimes it signifies the most high, perfect, and infinite being, who is of himself alone, and owes neither his being nor authority, nor anything to another; and this is what is most commonly intended when we speak of "God" in ordinary discourse, and in prayer and praise; we mean "God" in the highest sense.

At other times it has a lower sense and is made a title for persons who are invested with subordinate authority and power from that supreme being. Thus, angels are styled "gods."[3] "Thou hast made him a little lower than the gods," as it is in the margin;[4] so also, magistrates are "gods."[5] And sometimes in the singular number, one person is called "god," as Moses is twice so-called, a "god" to Aaron, and afterwards a "god" to Pharaoh.[6] And thus the devil is called "the god of this world," i.e., the prince and mighty ruler of it, though by unjust usurpation and God's permission.[7]

---

[3] Psalm 97:7.

[4] Psalm 8:5. Most English translations don't use the word "gods" in this verse. Thus the NRSV: "Yet you have made them a little lower than God, and crowned them with glory and honor." But the word translated as "God" is the Hebrew *elohim*, which is plural in form, and can mean "God" or "gods"—usually the context clarifies which is meant, although this verse in an exception. Thus, the NRSV footnote says "Or *than the divine beings* or *angels*"—or equivalently, "gods," as in the margin of the translation Emlyn is looking at.

[5] Exodus 22:28; Psalm 82:1; John 10:34–35.

[6] Exodus 4:16, 7:1.

[7] 2 Corinthians 4:4.

CHAPTER 1: GOD AND JESUS

Now, as he who alone is "God" in the former sense is infinitely above all these, so we find him distinguished from all others who are called "god" by the title "a God of gods,"[8] or the chief of all gods, with whom none of those gods may be compared.[9] So Philo describes him to be not only the "God of

---

[8] Deuteronomy 10:17; Joshua 22:22.

[9] Third century theologian Origen (c. 185–c. 254) addressed complaints that he taught two gods by distinguishing between different sorts of deity and corresponding uses of the word "god": "Many people who wish to be pious are troubled because they are afraid that they may proclaim two gods and, for this reason, they fall into false and impious beliefs. They either deny that the individual nature of the Son is other than that of the Father by confessing him to be God whom they refer to as 'Son' in name at least, or they deny the divinity of the Son and make his individual nature and essence as an individual to be different from the Father. Their problem can be resolved in this way. We must say to them that at one time "God" (with the article [Greek: *ho theos*]) is true God, wherefore also the Savior says in his prayer to the Father, 'That they may know you the only true God.' [John 17:3] On the other hand, everything besides the true God, which is made a god by participation in his divinity, would more properly not be said to be 'the god,' but 'a god.' To be sure, his 'firstborn of every creature' [Colossians 1:15], inasmuch as he was the first to be with God and has drawn divinity into himself, is more honored than the other gods beside him (of whom God is god as it is said, 'The God of gods, the Lord has spoken, and he has called the earth.' [Psalm 50:1, LXX] It was by his ministry that they became gods, for he drew from God that they might be deified, sharing ungrudgingly also with them according to his goodness. The God [Greek: *ho theos*], therefore, is the true God. The others are gods formed according to him as images of the prototype." Origen, *Commentary*, 98–99, translation modified (2.16–18). Writing in the first half of the first century CE, Jewish theologian Philo of Alexandria (fl. 30s CE) contrasts God with the visible stars in the sky, widely regarded by ancient people as deities: "We must, therefore, look on all those bodies in the heaven, which

men" but the "God of gods" also.¹⁰ This is the highest and most glorious title given to him in the Old Testament, when it is designed to make a most magnificent mention of his peerless greatness and glory.¹¹ I take that title to be equivalent to these which are so often used in the New Testament: "the God and Father of our Lord Jesus Christ," "the God of our Lord Jesus, the Father of Glory."¹² For since Jesus Christ is the chief of all subordinate powers, "the prince of the kings of the earth,"¹³ and far above the greatest angels,¹⁴ "the Lord of Lords, and King of Kings,"¹⁵ he who is called "the God of our Lord Jesus Christ,"¹⁶ is therein, in effect said to be "the God of gods" or above all gods.

---

the outward sense regards as gods, not as independent rulers, since they are assigned the work of lieutenants, being by their intrinsic nature responsible to a higher power, but by reason of their virtue not actually called to render in an account of their doings. So that, transcending all visible essence by means of our reason, let us press forward to the honour of that everlasting and invisible Being who can be comprehended and appreciated by the mind alone; who is not only the God of all gods, whether appreciable only by the intellect or visible to the outward senses, but is also the creator of them all. And if any one gives up the service due to the everlasting and uncreated God, transferring it to any more modern and created being, let him be set down as mad and as liable to the charge of the greatest impiety." Philo, *The Special Laws* I, 535 (1.19-20).

[10] Philo, *The Decalogue*, 521 (10.41).
[11] Psalm 86:8, 135:5.
[12] Ephesians 1:3, 17.
[13] Revelation 1:5.
[14] Ephesians 1:21.
[15] Revelation 17:14.
[16] Ephesians 1:17.

CHAPTER 1: GOD AND JESUS

Now the question to be resolved is, in which of these two senses is Christ said to be "god" in the holy Scriptures? Just the title "god" determines nothing in this case because it belongs both to the supreme and to subordinate beings in power and authority. The question is whether Jesus Christ is "the God of gods," or above all gods.

He is indeed the "Lord of lords," but that indicates an inferior description, compared with that of "God of gods," as appears in 1 Corinthians 8:5, though it be included in the superior, so that he who is above all gods is also over all lords, but not vice versa.[17] In short, does Jesus Christ have any god over him who has greater authority and greater ability than himself or not? This will decide the matter, for if he should have a god above him, then he is not the absolutely supreme god, though in relation to created beings he may be a "god" (or ruler) over all.[18]

---

[17] *W:* For this purpose are the words of that eminent philosopher Sir Isaac Newton in his *Optics* (pp. 314–5, Latin edition): "The word 'deity' implies exercise of dominion over subordinate beings, and though the word 'god' most frequently signifies 'lord,' yet every lord is not a god. The exercise of dominion in a spiritual being constitutes a god; if that dominion be real, that being is a real god; if it be fictitious, a false god; if it be supreme, the supreme god." He might have added: if subordinate, a subordinate god.

[18] *W:* Is not he alone "the one God," who knows "no superior," no cause of his existence, whom the Son himself teaches us to esteem "the only true God," and confesses to be "greater than himself," even "his God"? Eusebius, *On Ecclesiastical Theology*, 173–76 (1.11). See also Irenaeus, who frequently distinguishes the Father by this description: "the god over whom there is no other god." Irenaeus, *Against Heresies*, 419 (3.6.4).

CHAPTER I: GOD AND JESUS

I.2 *Jesus on Himself as Distinct from and Subordinate to God*

Nor can we more clearly prove this point than by showing first that Jesus Christ explicitly speaks of another "God" than himself. Secondly, that he considers this "God" to be above or over himself. Thirdly, that he lacks those supereminent and infinite perfections which belong only to the Lord God of gods. I shall discuss these in a manner suited to ordinary abilities, for I think it inappropriate to speak or write of important doctrines (which the common people must *believe* and must so far understand) in such a manner as leaves them wholly unintelligible.

First, our Lord Jesus Christ expressly speaks of another "God" distinct from himself; several times we find him saying "my God" of another: "My God, my God, why have you forsaken me?"[19] Surely he didn't mean to say, "Myself, myself, why have you forsaken me?" This "God" Jesus was addressing, then, was distinct from himself, as he declares in other places: "He shall know my doctrine, whether it be of God, or whether I speak of myself."[20] So John 8:42, where it is to be noted that he does not distinguish him from himself as "the Father," but rather as "God";[21] and therefore, in all

---

[19] Matthew 27:46. Compare: John 20:17.
[20] John 7:17.
[21] "Jesus said to them, 'If God were your Father, you would love me, for I came from God and now I am here. I did not come on my own, but he

CHAPTER I: GOD AND JESUS

reasonable interpretation, he cannot be supposed to be that self-same god from whom he distinguishes and to whom he opposes himself. How manifestly are the one God and the one Lord distinguished in 1 Corinthians 8:6?[22] And that there may be no good reason to say with Placaeus[23] that the "God and the Lord," or the cause from which all things are and the cause by or through which they are, are just two things said of the same one god, we may see them more clearly distinguished in Ephesians 4:5-6.[24] Here, since other things are put between the one Lord and one God, namely "one faith, one baptism," evidently these were *not* intended as two descriptions of the same being. I think that no one who impartially considers the scriptural records can doubt whether God and his Christ are two distinct beings.[25]

---

sent me.'" John 8:42.

[22] "Hence, as to the eating of food offered to idols, we know that 'no idol in the world really exists,' and that 'there is no God but one.' Indeed, even though there may be so-called gods in heaven or on earth—as in fact there are many gods and many lords—yet for us there is one God, the Father, from whom are all things and for whom we exist, and one Lord, Jesus Christ, through whom are all things and through whom we exist." 1 Corinthians 8:4-6.

[23] French Reformed theologian Joshua (or Josué) De La Place (Latinized as "Placaeus") (d. 1655).

[24] "There is one body and one Spirit, just as you were called to the one hope of your calling, one Lord, one faith, one baptism, one God and Father of all, who is above all and through all and in all." (Ephesians 4:4-6)

[25] By "beings" here Emlyn means individual realities; hence in his 1702 version he writes "two distinct things."

CHAPTER 1: GOD AND JESUS

Secondly, our Lord Jesus holds not only that another than himself is God, but also that this one is above or over himself, which is plainly indicated also by his apostles. Jesus himself loudly proclaims his subjection to the Father in many instances; in general he declares his Father to be greater than him.[26] He says that he came not in his own but in his Father's name or authority,[27] that he sought not his own but God's glory, and that he made not his own will but rather God's his rule.[28] And in such a posture of subjection "he came down from heaven" into this earth,[29] so that it should seem that this nature which pre-existed did not possess the supreme will, even before it was incarnate.[30] Again, he acknowledges his

---

[26] John 14:28; 10:29.

[27] John 5:43.

[28] John 5:30.

[29] John 6:38.

[30] As what many call an "Arian" (see note 1) Emlyn believes that Jesus pre-existed his human career; hence, his reference to the "nature" (i.e. being) which existed before Jesus' human life. In his biographical note Emlyn's son explains that Emlyn and his friend, Protestant minister William Manning, "were both of an inquisitive temper" and were drawn into thinking about the Trinity by reading some of the literature from the famous controversy among Anglicans from 1689 to 1698. (On this see Dixon, *Nice and Hot*, chapters 4–5.) After much thought, "Mr. Manning took the Socinian way, and strove hard to bring Mr. Emlyn into that way of thinking, but Mr. Emlyn never could be brought to doubt either of the pre-existence of our Saviour, as the Logos, or that God created the material world by him. Upon these points they had many friendly debates . . . but the Socinian interpretation appeared to our author [i.e. Emlyn] so forced and unnatural that he could by no means give in to it." Emlyn, "Memoirs," xiii–xiv, modernized.

CHAPTER I: GOD AND JESUS

dependence upon his God and Father, even concerning those things which some suppose belong to him as God, namely the power of working miracles, of raising the dead, and of executing universal judgment—about all of which he says, "Of my own self I can do nothing."[31] In like manner his apostles declare his subjection to another, not only as his Father, but as his God, which is emphatically expressed, in calling the most blessed God "the God of our Lord Jesus," after his humiliation was over.[32] Again, Paul says that the "head of Christ is God."[33] They declare Christ's headship over the universe, and the very foundations of his claim to honor and service, to be due to the gracious gift of God, *echarisato auto* ["granted him"][34] and yet these are some of the highest glories of Jesus Christ.

Let me only add to this topic that great text, so full of irresistible evidence for the inferiority of the Son to his Father (or to God), 1 Corinthians 15:24–29,[35] where the apostle says several relevant things.

---

[31] John 5: 19–20, 26–27, 30.

[32] Ephesians 1:17.

[33] 1 Corinthians 11:3.

[34] Philippines 2:9.

[35] "Then comes the end, when he [Jesus] hands over the kingdom to God the Father, after he has destroyed every ruler and every authority and power. For he must reign until he has put all his enemies under his feet. The last enemy to be destroyed is death. For 'God has put all things in subjection under his feet.' [Psalm 8:6] But when it says, 'All things are put in subjection,' it is plain that this does not include the one who put all things in subjection under him. When all things are subjected to him, then the Son himself will also be subjected to the one who put all things in

CHAPTER 1: GOD AND JESUS

First, he says that all things are to be put under Christ's feet—all enemies and powers are to be subdued to him—but he adds that it is clear that God must be excluded from these things that are under him because it is he who put all under Christ. And why is it, that it is so clear, that *someone else* must be supposed to be the great author of this triumph of Christ? Why might it not be done by himself independently, if he is the supreme God? (Then there need have been no exclusion of any one from the "all things" under him.) But the apostle knew that Jesus Christ must triumph by a power derived from God, to whom that power was to be ascribed in the highest sense. To one who had such thoughts, it was clear that there must be one excluded from the "all things" under him, because one who enables Christ to subdue all things (who makes him a god over all), must be above him.[36]

Second, he says that the Son shall deliver up his kingdom to God, that is, to the Father, *not* to the Father, Son, and Holy Spirit, as some suppose, but to the Father only, since it was the

---

subjection under him, so that God may be all in all. Otherwise, what will those people do who receive baptism on behalf of the dead? If the dead are not raised at all, why are people baptized on their behalf?" 1 Corinthians 15:24–29.

[36] Emlyn may be referring here to Romans 9:5, in which some translations have Paul calling Jesus "God over all." (e.g. NIV, ESV) If so, then Emlyn's point would be that based on the passages discussed in this section, Paul could only mean that Christ is a god (i.e. rightful religious ruler over all other created beings) *under* God, so that the Son and the Father are *not* "god/God" in the same sense of the word. On whether or not this text calls Jesus "God" see Harris, *Jesus as God*, 143–72 (pro) and Schoenheit et. al., *One God*, 473-75, 606. (con).

CHAPTER 1: GOD AND JESUS

Father who gave him all power in heaven and earth, and who made him King in Zion.[37] Christ will surrender all into God's hands, in testimony of his having done all in subordination to him, and having acted and ruled in dependence on him who shall have a satisfactory account of all given to him in the end. This is a glory unique to the Father as supreme.

Third, he says, then the Son himself shall be subject to him who put all things under him—to God his Father—so that "God may be all in all." That is, his subjection shall be then manifested by an open and solemn acknowledgement of it, when he shall recognize the supremacy of the Father in that public act of surrender, so that though formerly (i.e. in the present state) all judgment and rule was committed to the Son, yet then it shall be otherwise, and God will more immediately appear in the government of the future state, which shall not be so much shared, probably between him and the Redeemer, as the present administration appears to be. This then will be the resolution of all our disputes: God all in all, and the Son himself subject under him. Can anything be more expressive of an inequality between God and Christ?

But it will be said by some, that the "Son" means the Son of Man, or Christ *as man*, while *as God*, he shall not be subjected to the Father.

Response: as there is no indication of any such distinction between the supposed two natures of the Son here, so there is enough in the words to show that they are spoken of him

---

[37] Matthew 28:18; Psalm 110:1–2; Ephesians 1:22; Hebrews 2:8.

under his highest capacity and description, so that Monsieur Claude[38] maintains it to be true of the Son of God as to his (supposed) divine nature. But though there is no need to suppose such a nature (which I think the text plainly contradicts) yet he proves why these words do speak of Christ under his highest description, the name of "Son." For first, as he says, it does not say the "Son of Man," but "the Son" absolutely, which he thinks in Scripture often means more than the "Son of Man." Undoubtedly, it implies all that comes under that title and even more, since it is said, "even the Son himself," with great emphasis, as if it should say that as great and glorious as he is, with all his grandeur and power, he himself shall be subject. Secondly, his subjection being contrasted with his reign, both must be understood of the same subject. Surely, the delivering up of the kingdom can only be done by the same to which it was committed, and by which it was managed. Now I grant that Christ could give up his kingdom only in his human nature, but then it is because it is as a man delegated and inhabited by God that he directs and manages this kingdom, and if this to be allowed (as I think it must) that the man Christ is sufficient, by help from God, to manage his universal spiritual kingdom, I see no reason to oppose those unitarians who think him to be a sufficient savior and prince even though he isn't the only supreme God. Nor can any, with reason, attempt to prove him to be such from his works and office as king of his church, since it is

---

[38] French Protestant minister Jean Claude (1619–87).

implied that as such he must do homage to God the Father in "delivering up his kingdom to him." And this very expression, "to God the Father," makes it plain, that there is no God the Son in the same sense, or in the same supreme essence with the Father, because if there were then he ought not to be excluded from his glory of having such open homage paid to him, which is here given to the Father only. And since the apostle speaks of the same God (whom he explains to be the Father) throughout this discourse, and says he shall be "all in all," how clearly does he show him to be far beyond all that are not God the Father, whatever other descriptions apply to them? So then, Jesus Christ, in his highest capacity, being inferior to the Father, how can he be the same god to whom he is subject, or of the same rank and dignity?

Thus it appears that Christ is "God" insofar as he is under a *superior* god, who has set him over all. This fits with the scriptural explication of the deity of the blessed Jesus—that he is invested with a God-like authority and power from the supreme God his Father. Thus, when he was accused by the fault-finding Jews of assuming the title "the Son of God" (which they would perversely stretch, as though it implied an equality with God) he explains in what sense he justified it, namely "as one whom the Father has sanctified," i.e. called to a greater office, and honored with a higher commission than those magistrates, on whom the Scripture so freely bestows the title of "gods."[39] So when he is called "God," it is explained

---

[39] John 10:35–36. For an analysis of the argument here see Tuggy, "Jesus's

in what sense or what sort of "God" he is.[40] It is to be understood that by saying *his* god (implying that he had a god over him) had "anointed him with oil," etc., that is, had invested him with royal power and dignity (as kings were installed in their office among the Jews by anointing with oil) which is an explication of his deity or dominion. And he is said to be "above his fellows," not, to be sure, above the Father and Holy Spirit (which are supposed by those who understand Jesus' deity to be the supreme deity to be his fellows as God) but above all other subordinate powers. This is one simple, scriptural explanation of his being called "God," for these things are spoken *to* him and *of* him under the title of "God"—"O God, your throne," etc.[41] I think people should be well assured on what grounds they go before they assign *other* reasons for this title being given to him which are so different from the scriptural explanation. Let it be enough for us that God has "made him both Lord and Christ," that he has "exalted him to be a Prince and a Savior."[42]

Our adversaries will gain nothing by prooftexts in which the title of "God" is given to Christ,[43] since that may be, and

---

argument."

[40] "But of the Son he says, 'Your throne, O God, is forever and ever, and the righteous scepter is the scepter of your kingdom. You have loved righteousness and hated wickedness; therefore God, your God, has anointed you with the oil of gladness beyond your companions." Hebrews 1:8–9

[41] Hebrews 1:8.

[42] Acts 2:36; 5:31.

[43] An important recent study of the word *theos* being used to refer to

yet it will not prove him to be the supreme and independent God, but only one who is inhabited and commissioned and enabled by him who is so. As to that place which is corruptly rendered in our translation, "he thought it no robbery to be equal with God,"[44] it is confessed by our adversaries themselves, that it should be read thus: that he did not assume, or arrogate, or snatch at an equality with God, or covet to appear in the likeness of God.[45] The words are never known to be used in any other sense, as is shown by Dr. Tillotson in his discourses against the Socinians,[46] also by Dr. Whitby in his exposition on that text, and others.[47] So that this rather denies than asserts Christ's equality to God, though he was "in the form of God," as that has to do with the outward resemblance of him in his mighty power and works, etc.,

---

Jesus in the New Testament is Harris, *Jesus as God*.

[44] Philippians 2:6.

[45] *W*: One reason why I think what we render "to be equal with God" may be translated "to be like to God" is that the word *isos* ["equal to"] admits degrees of comparison, *isoteros, isotatos* ["more equal to," "most equal to"]. Now a strict arithmetical equality does not admit degrees, and no things can be more or less *equal*, than what are exactly so. But things may be more or less *alike*, and though things that are alike may be equal, they are not hereby proved or said to be so. See Dr. Whitby's discussion; he gives several examples where the word *isos* ["equal to"] is so used (Whitby, *A Paraphrase*, 338).

[46] Tillotson, *Sermon 54*, 396. The sermons of Anglican Archbishop John Tillotson (1630–94) were widely ready in Emyln's day.

[47] Daniel Whitby (1638–1726) was an Arminian Anglican priest and theologian who by the end of his life came to hold a unitarian view of God, on which see Whitby, *The Last Thoughts*.

CHAPTER I: GOD AND JESUS

which is the constant meaning of the word "form" in the New Testament.

But because some think perfections are ascribed to Christ in Scripture which will prove him to be God in the highest sense, I proceed to show next that our blessed Lord Jesus disavows those infinite perfections which belong only to the supreme God of gods. And it is most certain that if he lacks *any* of these perfections that are essential to the Deity, he is not "God" in the primary sense. And if we can find him disavowing the one, he cannot lay claim to the other, for to deny himself to have all the divine perfections, or to deny himself to be the infinite God, is the same thing.

CHAPTER 2: The Human Jesus

2.1 *How Jesus Denies Having Divine Attributes*

ONE GREAT AND UNIQUE PERFECTION of the Deity is absolute, underived omnipotence. He who cannot work all miracles and do whatever he chooses *on his own*, without help from another, can never be the supreme being, or God, because he appears to be a defective being, comparatively, since he needs help and can receive additional strength from someone else.

Now it is most evident that our Lord Jesus (whatever power he had) confesses again and again, that he did not have infinite power on his own: "Of myself I can do nothing."[48] He had been speaking of great miracles, namely, raising the dead, and carrying out all judgment, but all along he takes care that we should know that his sufficiency for these things was from

---

[48] John 5:30.

God the Father. In the beginning of the discourse, he says, "The Son can do nothing but what he sees the Father do."[49] And in the middle, "The Father has given to the Son to have life in himself."[50] And as if he could never too much impress this great truth on our minds, he adds towards the conclusion, "I can do nothing of myself" (Greek: *ap emautou*),[51] or, from nothing that is myself do I draw this power and authority. Surely this is *not* the voice of God, but of a man! For the Most High can receive from no one;[52] he cannot be made more mighty or wise, etc., because no addition can be made to absolute perfection. And since power in God is an essential perfection, it follows that if it is derived, then so is the essence or being itself, which is blasphemy against the Most High, for it is to un-god him, to number him among dependent, derivative beings. But the supreme God indeed is only he who is the First Cause and absolute source of all.

Furthermore, our Lord speaks of himself here in contrast to his Father, who he says gave him all power. Now if he had such an eternal divine Word united more nearly to him than the Father, surely he would have admitted his power to be from that Word or divine Son. How can it be that he ascribes nothing to that, since this Word is supposed to be equal in power to the Father himself, and more nearly allied to Jesus

---

[49] John 5:19.
[50] John 5:26.
[51] John 5:30.
[52] "Who has ever given to God, that God should repay them?" Romans 11:35 (NIV).

CHAPTER 2: THE HUMAN JESUS

Christ as the operating agent in him? He says instead that "My Father in me does the works,"[53] by which it is clear there was no divine agent in and with him except the Father, who alone has all power of himself and needs no assistance.

Another infinite perfection that must be in the Deity is supreme, absolute goodness. All nations have consented to this by the light of nature, that the Greek *to agathon* (The Good) and the Latin *optimus maximus* (Best and Greatest), are the main titles of the Supreme. As the orator says, he is one *quo nec melius, nec majus concipi potest* ("than whom nothing better, nothing greater can be conceived")[54]—the fullest, and highest of all that are called "good"—for indeed all other goodness is derived from him.

But the Lord Jesus explicitly disavows this description "good": "Jesus said to him, 'Why do you call me good? There is none good but one, that is God.' "[55] Here it is most evident that he distinguishes himself from God as not the same with him and denies of himself what he affirms of God. And as to that divine perfection of supreme, infinite goodness, he challenges the man for presuming to say words which seemed to attribute it to him, and leads him off to another who alone is "good" in a higher sense.[56]

---

[53] John 14:10.

[54] Emlyn here seems to paraphrase a point made by Roman rhetorician Marcus Tullius Cicero (106–43 BCE); see Cicero, *Nature*, 54 (2.18).

[55] Mark 10:18; Matthew 19:17; Luke 18:19.

[56] *W*: Origen, *Against Celsus*, 72 (5.11); *On First Principles*, 65 (1.2.13).

CHAPTER 2: THE HUMAN JESUS

It's astonishing to see what violence is done to the sacred text by those who maintain the equality of Jesus Christ to God his Father. How strange it is to suppose that our Lord's meaning is: "I know, man, you do not understand me to be God, as I am. Why, then, do you give me the title belonging to him only?" There is not one word in the context which suggests this. Christ never challenges the poor man with this, that he thought *too lowly* of Jesus (as they suppose), but quite to the contrary, that he thought or spoke *too highly* of him. And truly, if the man's error was thinking too lowly of Christ, while his words otherwise were fairly enough applied to him, I cannot think our Lord would have rebuked him in that manner. For instead of keeping him still on the right subject and correcting his wrong conceptions about it, he seems clearly to carry him off to another from himself, as *not* the right subject, without correcting his thoughts *of Christ* at all. And for what purpose could Christ rebuke him in such a way that he never tells him what his mistake was, but rather tempts him to run astray into another mistake?

But rather than thinking too lowly of Christ, it'd make more sense (if anyone back then actually thought this) that the man thought Jesus to be God. For if he thought Jesus to be the *supreme* good, that is to think of him as God. (If he only meant that Jesus was a less-than-supreme good, how could Christ rebuke him for it, since that would reflect no fault or error? And of course, those who say Christ's receiving worship while

CHAPTER 2: THE HUMAN JESUS

on earth proves his deity[57] can't explain why this man should give or why Christ should receive worship, as we see in Mark 10:17, unless he thought Christ was God.) But whatever the man thought, he said what Jesus Christ thought was only properly said about God and which was too much to be said about himself, as the obvious sense of his words declares.

Let me add, that if our Lord Jesus on purpose left the matter unclear, not willing to reveal who he was at that time, then it is strange that the evangelists, who many years afterward relate the matter, when it was necessary for people to believe (as it is supposed) that Christ was supreme God, should not clarify the matter by inserting some cautious clause, such as that Christ said this to test the man, or because he knew the man denied his deity, or the like, for sometimes on lesser occasions they give such cautions.[58] But even though three of the evangelists relate this discourse, they all do it the same way, and not one of them gives us the slightest hint to direct us to the secret way of interpretation, but leaves us liable to a most fatal mistake (even recommended to us by this report) *if* Jesus Christ were indeed the supreme Good in as high a sense as God his Father, which he apparently denies here, and by that denies himself to be the most high God.

I will only add one perfection more, namely, absolute omniscience, or unlimited knowledge of all things, past,

---

[57] For Emlyn's view on the worship of Christ, see Emlyn's section 3.2 below, pp. 90-97.
[58] John 6:6; John 21:23.

CHAPTER 2: THE HUMAN JESUS

present, and to come. "His understanding is infinite."[59] "Known to God are all his works from the beginning."[60]

Now it's clear that our Lord Jesus Christ lacked this infinite knowledge, particularly about future things, such as the day of judgment. He says, "Of that day knows no man, no, not the angels of heaven, nor the Son, but the Father only."[61] Here, the Son professes his knowledge to be limited and inferior to the Father's, and this limited one is "the Son" of the Father (i.e. of God), the Son who is above angels when it comes to knowledge, the "Son" in the highest sense.[62] Now, how is it possible that the Son should be infinite, and yet have only a finite understanding?[63] Or can he be equal in

---

[59] Psalm 147:5. Compare: Isaiah 41:23.

[60] "Known unto God are all his works from the beginning of the world." Acts 15:18 (KJV). The verse is shorter in recent translations because they are based on recent critical editions of the Greek, e.g. "known from long ago." (NRSV)

[61] Mark 13:32. See also Matthew 24:36.

[62] Emlyn here is heading off the traditional dodge of saying that Jesus was limited in knowledge "as human" but infinite in knowledge "as divine."

[63] Sollom Emlyn inserts a marginal comment here referring to Irenaeus's *Against Heresies*, written around 180 CE. There, like many other early authors, Irenaeus shows that he accepts Jesus' claim of ignorance at face value. In the context, Irenaeus is defending his claim that the Son's "generation" by the Father is "altogether indescribable," so that neither he nor anyone else can say how it is or by what means the Father does this. Irenaeus writes that "even the Lord Jesus, the very Son of God, allowed that the Father alone knows the very day and hour of judgment, when He plainly declares, 'But of that day and that hour knoweth no man, neither the Son, but the Father only.' [Translators' note: Mark 13:32. The words

CHAPTER 2: THE HUMAN JESUS

knowledge to the Father, and yet not know as much as the Father? To be sure, if he was not an infinite god when on the earth he cannot be such afterwards. Thus we have seen Christ himself with his own mouth disavowing infinite and underived power, goodness, and knowledge. He attributes these to the Father only, as to another who is distinct from himself, and from whom he derived each in a dependent and limited manner.

2.2 *Why "Two-Natures" Speculations Don't Help*

What can be said against these clear arguments? I imagine our opponents have only one move left for evading them, and that is a distinction which serves them in all cases: they say Jesus Christ says these things about himself "as man only," while he had another nature "as God," which he reserved and excepted out of the case, so that when he says "I cannot do this myself," or "I am not to be called the chief good," or "I do not know this," etc., according to them, the meaning is: "I don't have these perfections *in my human nature,* nonetheless I know

---

'neither the angels which are in heaven,' are here omitted, probably because, as usual, the writer quotes from memory.] If then, the Son was not ashamed, to ascribe the knowledge of that day to the Father only, but declared what was true regarding the matter, neither let us be ashamed to reserve for God those greater questions which may occur to us." Irenaeus, *Against Heresies*, 401 (2.28.6).

CHAPTER 2: THE HUMAN JESUS

and can do all unassisted, and am the chief good *in my divine nature*, which also is more properly myself."[64]

I intend now to expose the futility of this tricky move by showing how absurd it is to suppose that this distinction of two natures removes the force of such expressions from Christ's own mouth which in their natural and ordinary appearance proclaim his inferiority to God, even the Father. And I shall dwell more on this because it's the most popular and common evasion, and comes in at every turn, when all other relief fails.

It's reasonable for us to ask what hint of such a distinction of two natures they can point us to in any of these discourses of Christ. Should we devise or imagine for him such a strange and seemingly deceitful way of speaking simply to uphold our own precarious opinion? But I have several remarks to make about this common answer.

---

[64] Emlyn here makes an astute point about traditional "two natures" christological speculations. It looks like they must say that the Son of God is personally identical to (i.e. is the same self as) "the divine nature," a.k.a. the Word of John 1:1. In contrast, they can't say that he's the same self as "the human nature," the body-soul composite or the man, since they want to say that the Son existed a long time before this composite, human-divine thing or this only human thing existed. Hence his comment that for a two-natures theory, it is the divine nature which is "more properly" Jesus. It is unclear, though, why one should suppose that an eternal divine nature who has "assumed" (mysteriously united to) a human type of body and a human type of soul (or even a man) amounts to a real human being. For this and other difficulties with two natures speculations see Tuggy, "Clarifying Catholic Christologies," Tuggy, "podcast 165," and Tuggy, "podcast 166."

CHAPTER 2: THE HUMAN JESUS

My first objection is that our blessed Lord Jesus Christ, if he was the supreme God in any nature of his own, he could not have said, it seems to me, consistently with truth and sincerity (which he always maintained strictly), that he could *not* do or did *not* know something which all this while he himself *could* do or *did* know very well—as surely as if he were the supreme God, he could and did. This would be to make him say what is most false and to equivocate in the most deceitful manner. Even if we should suppose he consisted of two infinitely distant natures, and so had two capacities of knowing and acting, yet since he includes them both, it follows that when he denies something of himself in absolute terms, without any limitation in the words or other obvious circumstances, he plainly implies a denial of its belonging to any part of his person, or any nature in it. Although we may affirm a thing of a person which belongs only to a part of him, as I may properly say a man is wounded or hurt, though it only be in one part, suppose, an arm—yet I cannot rightly deny a thing of him which belongs only to one part, because it belongs not to another. I can't say a man is not wounded because although one arm is shot or wounded yet the other is unharmed. For instance, I have two organs of sight, two eyes. Now suppose I converse with a man with one eye shut and the other open. If being asked whether I saw him, I should dare to say that I didn't see him (without any qualification) meaning (to myself) that I didn't see him with the eye which was shut although I saw him well enough with the eye which was open, I fear I would be criticized as a liar and deceiver, notwithstanding such a mental reservation as some would attribute to the holy Jesus. For knowledge is the eye of the person; Jesus Christ is supposed to have two of these knowing capacities, the one weak, the other strong and piercing, discerning all things. Now as such a one, the disciples come to him and ask him when the end of the world and time of his coming shall be.[65] He answers them by giving them some general account of the matter, but says that he didn't know the particular day and hour, nor did any know them except the Father, meaning (say my opponents) that it wasn't included in his human knowledge, although he knew it well enough with his divine nature, at the same time that he said absolutely and without qualification that the Son doesn't know it.

If Jesus Christ had a divine knowledge and nature, no doubt his disciples (who, if anyone, must have believed it) would have directed their question to that divine capacity of his rather than to the imperfect human capacity, and yet in answer to their question he says he didn't know the day, which would not be counted as sincere or truthful in ordinary people. But surely we mustn't think Jesus Christ was dishonest in this way, for in his mouth was no guile.[66] Let us not impute it to him.

---

[65] Matthew 24:3.
[66] "For even hereunto were ye called: because Christ also suffered for us, leaving us an example, that ye should follow his steps: Who did no sin, neither was guile found in his mouth: Who, when he was reviled, reviled not again; when he suffered, he threatened not; but committed himself to

CHAPTER 2: THE HUMAN JESUS

That you may see this is good reasoning, hear how some of the other side admit it when out of the heat of this controversy. See Dr. Stillingfleet's sermon on Matthew 10:16[67] on the equivocation of Catholic priests whose common answer, when questioned about what they have known by hearing confession, is that they *don't* know it. And they think it vindicates them from the charge of lying to say that in confession the priest knows matters "as God,[68] not as man," and therefore he denies knowing them, meaning "as man."[69] But, says the Doctor, this is absurd, because to say he does not know is as much as to say that he does not *in any way* know.[70] Now if this is a good answer against the Catholics, as no doubt it is, then it surely is so in the present case.

---

him that judgeth righteously: Who his own self bare our sins in his own body on the tree, that we, being dead to sins, should live unto righteousness: by whose stripes ye were healed." 1 Peter 2:21–24 (KJV).

[67] Stillingfleet, *Fifty Sermons*, 253–73. Edward Stillingfleet (1635–99) was an Arminian Anglican bishop of Worcester who was famous as a prolific controversial writer.

[68] That is, as God's representative. See Stillingfleet, *Fifty Sermons*, 268.

[69] In late medieval and early modern Roman Catholicism, many scholars argued that it was permissible to say something one knew to be false, for instance, a priest denying knowledge of something he heard in confession, so long as one had a "mental reservation," a modifying phrase in one's mind which when added to what was actually said would make it a true statement. This was widely criticized, especially in Protestant countries. But in 1679 a Pope condemned this teaching as "scandalous and pernicious in practice" (Innocent XI, *A Decree*, Preface, 7) and in recent times it plays no part in Catholic moral teaching.

[70] Stillingfleet, *Fifty Sermons*, 265.

CHAPTER 2: THE HUMAN JESUS

Therefore, when Christ says he doesn't know the day of judgment, it is as much as to say that he does not *in any way* know it, and consequently it is a useless trick to say that his ignorance was "as man only." We must beware lest we make the holy Jesus as liable to the charge of equivocation as are the Catholic priests, and lest we make the Jesuits think they have a good claim to that name[71] because in their practice of lying they are imitating Jesus' example—a great advantage, they imagine, of this "mental reservation" interpretation of his denying knowing the day or hour.

As a further evidence that Jesus Christ intended no such distinction of two natures, as is supposed, it's to be observed that he doesn't distinguish between the Son of Man and the eternal Word (as some would) but between the Son and his Father; the Son doesn't know, but only the Father.[72] Thus it is clear that he had no thought of including any person or nature of his own among those excluded by his phrase "only the Father." For whatever was not the Father, he says was ignorant of that day. Now it's certain that in no nature was the Son the Father, and consequently where no one but the Father knows, no one who is not the Father can be intended. And since our Lord was making an exception in the case, he would not have forgotten to except the eternal Word too, if there had been such a divine agent in himself, equal to the Father and

---

[71] That is, The Society of Jesus (the full name of the Jesuit religious order).

[72] "But about that day or hour no one knows, neither the angels in heaven, nor the Son, but only the Father." Mark 13:32.

distinct from him. For it's a known rule that an exception from a general assertion confirms that general assertion in other instances not excepted.[73]

Will they say that "the Father" here means all three Persons, Father, Son, and Holy Spirit? What?! Can "the Father," as opposed to "the Son," mean both the Father and the Son? What woeful work will this make with Scripture, to suppose that things opposed to each other are included in each other because of the very titles by which they are opposed? They may as well say that in the baptismal formula,[74] by "the Father" is meant "Father, Son, and Spirit," though he be distinguished from the other two. And I should despair of ever understanding the Scriptures above all books that were written at this rate of interpretation. There is no doubt, therefore, that "the Father," as opposed to "the Son," excludes all that is the Son. Thus, there can be no Son of God who knew of that day which only the Father knew of, and consequently no Son that is God equal to the Father.

Moreover, that interpretation must be unreasonable, which if admitted would make even the clearest statements uncertain and utterly meaningless, as this interpretation of

---

[73] Emlyn's point is put abstractly here, but an example makes his point clear. If you say, "All the apples in the basket except these two are rotten," you are asserting rottenness of all the other apples in the basket, all of them beyond these two exceptions. Thus, when Jesus says that *only* the Father knows the day and hour, he is asserting that anyone other than the Father fails to know the day and hour.

[74] Matthew 28:19.

CHAPTER 2: THE HUMAN JESUS

Christ's words would do. I ask the patrons of this opinion: in what words could Jesus Christ have straightforwardly denied himself to be God Most High, if he had a mind to do it, more clearly and fully than these, in which he says that he didn't know all things, as the Father did, nor could do all things, etc? I would like them to show me what words of that sort he could have used, which the same way of interpretation as they use here will not evade and make meaningless. For had he said, or sworn in plain words, saying, "I tell you I am not the supreme God, and none but my Father has that glory," they would for the same reason still have said that this was to be understood of him "as man only." If this method of interpretation were to be allowed then no words professing himself not to be God could be a proof of it. I may therefore safely say this much, that the blessed Jesus has declared himself *not* to be the supreme God, or equal to the Father, as clearly as words can speak or briefly express, and that this declaration made by him already can be evaded only at the cost of making it impossible for him to say such a thing using any words whatever. Let anyone test this to see if it holds true; surely, it must be an absurd way of interpretation, which leaves a man no opportunity or power of speaking his meaning clearly, so as to be understood.

Again, this way of interpretation, which the advocates of the opinion I oppose need so badly to uphold their cause, clearly overthrows it again, and may be turned against them. For if it be reasonable and true to deny of Christ absolutely what belongs to him in one nature, because there is another

CHAPTER 2: THE HUMAN JESUS

nature in which it doesn't belong to him, then since to be the chief God belongs to him (according to our adversaries) only in one nature and not in respect of the other (or human) nature, it follows that it may as rightly be said that "Jesus Christ is not God, nor to be worshiped or trusted as such," even that "he did not exist before the virgin Mary," according to them, and the like. And we could say this without adding any limitation or restriction, any more than our Lord Jesus does in the place mentioned.[75]

What would they say to one who should speak or preach that Jesus is not God, that he cannot do all things, nor is he equal to the Father, etc.? Would they not concede that such a person was a denier of the deity of Christ, otherwise he would never say such things? For the same reason, when Jesus Christ himself says that he cannot of himself do all things, nor knows all things, making no verbal qualifications, we may conclude that he also denies that he is the supreme God—otherwise, if it is an accurate way of speaking for him, it can't be inaccurate for us to imitate him by simply denying him to be what he is not in one of his natures, i.e. that he is not God, without adding more.

Moreover, by following this way of speaking which they attribute to Christ, a man may be taught to say his creed backwards, and yet make a true profession of his faith, by denying of Jesus Christ, in absolute expressions, whatever may be denied of one of his natures. Thus, since the Apostles'

---

[75] Mark 13:32.

CHAPTER 2: THE HUMAN JESUS

Creed[76] mentions nothing to be believed concerning Christ except what belongs to his human nature (which would be strange, if there were any required doctrines relating to his supreme deity, which must be most important), one may venture to deny them all, with this secret, unexpressed qualification, namely, meaning it of the divine nature (to which they don't belong). In this way one may say, "I believe that Jesus Christ was *not* conceived by the Holy Spirit or born of the virgin Mary; I believe that he never was crucified under Pontius Pilate, nor was he ever dead or buried. I believe that he never rose nor ascended, nor will he return visibly again." For his divine nature (which it's supposed that he had) was not capable of these things. And since they say that his personhood is divine, there seems all the more reason to be bolder in denying without qualification of the person what does not belong to the divine nature whose the personhood is, than in denying of the person what only doesn't belong to the human nature, as this interpretation makes Christ to do.

---

[76] The so-called Apostles' Creed reached its final form sometime in the Middle Ages, but it is similar to many short creeds of the first three Christian centuries. It reads, "I believe in God the Father almighty, creator of heaven and earth; And in Jesus Christ, His only Son, our Lord, Who was conceived by the Holy Spirit, born of the Virgin Mary, suffered under Pontius Pilate, was crucified, dead and buried. He descended to hell, on the third day rose again from the dead, ascended to heaven, sits at the right hand of God the Father almighty, thence He will come to judge the living and the dead; I believe in the Holy Spirit, the holy catholic Church, the communion of saints, the forgiveness of sins, the resurrection of the body [*carnis*], and the life everlasting. Amen." "*Textus Receptus*," 24–25.

CHAPTER 2: THE HUMAN JESUS

Finally, it seems significant to me, in opposition to this way of interpretation, that the evangelists never take any occasion (when they had so many) to add any warning against taking Christ's words in their obvious sense, when he says that he did not know the hour, and the like. If, as is said, our Lord didn't intend to reveal his divinity (although I still don't see why he should deny it in this way), nevertheless his apostles, who wrote so many years after and intended to reveal all important truths most clearly, would not fail to have guided the reader by removing such obvious objections against the supreme deity of Christ, and by saying that he said this only in respect of his human nature, that he didn't know all things, etc. But there is not one warning given, as often we find they gave about lesser matters.[77] No doubt it was because they wanted Jesus' words to be understood at face value, not thinking of any such secret qualification in Christ's mind, of a divine nature in his person which is an implied exception, when he had denied such perfections of his person without qualification.

---

[77] For example: "Jesus answered them, 'Destroy this temple, and in three days I will raise it up.' The Jews then said, 'This temple has been under construction for forty-six years, and will you raise it up in three days?' [Warning:] But he was speaking of the temple of his body." John 2:19–22. And, "After saying this, he [i.e. Jesus] told them, 'Our friend Lazarus has fallen asleep, but I am going there to awaken him.' The disciples said to him, 'Lord, if he has fallen asleep, he will be all right.' [Warning:] Jesus, however, had been speaking about his death, but they thought that he was referring merely to sleep." John 11:11–13.

CHAPTER 2: THE HUMAN JESUS

Thus it remains good that Jesus Christ denies infinite perfections to belong to him as they belong to the Father, and therefore that he is not the same infinite God with him, if we can believe his own words. But before I conclude this argument, I shall endeavor to answer what our opposers offer on the contrary side. They say there is abundant evidence from *other* Scriptures that Jesus Christ has those perfections in him which I have showed in the aforementioned places he denies of himself. These they weigh against the other, and since both sides cannot be proved, we will have to determine which ought to yield. In particular, they say that omniscience is ascribed to Jesus Christ, the sort of knowledge which only the supreme God has. And since this indeed is that infinite perfection for which they seem to have the most plausible prooftexts, therefore I choose to focus on this in particular. I think I have proven the negative claim already from his own mouth, that he did *not* know all things, nor can anything of equal evidence and force be produced in favor of the affirmative claim, as will appear upon careful examination.

CHAPTER 3: Answering Objections

3.1 *Answering Scriptural Objections about Christ's Knowledge*

THE INSTANCES USUALLY ALLEGED to prove the infinite omniscience of Jesus Christ are either such as speak of his knowing "all things" in general or of his knowing human thoughts and hearts in particular.

For one thing, it's objected that the disciples ascribe to him the knowledge of all things, saying "You know all things."[78] I answer that those expressions are words of admiration from disciples who are not yet inspired, so they are intended only to express a very great and comprehensive knowledge, far from infinite divine omniscience, as appears from three considerations.

First, consider Christ's own words: he did not know what the Father knew, namely, the particular time of the day of judgment.[79]

---

[78] John 16:30; John 21:17.
[79] Matthew 24:36; Mark 13:32.

CHAPTER 3: ANSWERING OBJECTIONS

Second, it was common to ascribe "all" knowledge to men of extraordinary wisdom, especially when any intended to commend them highly and were struck with awe, for admiration and praise naturally tend towards hyperbole. Thus the woman of Tekoa, impressed with David's wisdom, cries out, "My Lord knows all things on earth, and is as wise as an angel."[80] And the apostle in commendation of some Christians says they "know all things."[81] And yet it's obvious that such accolades must have their limitations. Indeed, the Jews seem to have thought that their prophets know, in a manner, "all things." Thus, when a woman with a bad reputation anointed our Lord's head, the Pharisee says of him, "If this man were a prophet, he would know what manner of woman this is."[82] And when the Samaritan woman found that he told her all her secret acts that she ever did, she concludes thus: "Sir, I perceive you are a prophet."[83] It's no wonder, then, if the disciples speak thus of him, "You know all things," without esteeming him more than the greatest of prophets.

---

[80] 2 Samuel 14:20.

[81] "But you have been anointed by the Holy One, and all of you have knowledge. [Note: Other ancient authorities read *you know all things*] . . . As for you, the anointing that you received from him abides in you, and so you do not need anyone to teach you. But as his anointing teaches you about all things, and is true and is not a lie, and just as it has taught you, abide in him [Footnote: Or *abide in it*]." 1 John 2:20, 27.

[82] Luke 7:39.

[83] John 4:19, 29.

CHAPTER 3: ANSWERING OBJECTIONS

Third, it's evident that they never intended more by attributing "all knowledge" to him, from their own words in one of the texts mentioned, where the disciples tell us how much they inferred from his great knowledge (which they describe and extol by saying "You know all things")—not that he *was* God, but rather that he was *one sent by* God. "By this we believe that you came forth from God," not that you yourself are that God.[84] By these generous expressions they only intend to attribute to him what a created being is capable of by divine assistance. Therefore, it does violence to their words to infer from them that Jesus Christ is God when they themselves, who best knew their own meaning, infer no such thing.

And yet if it were granted that our Lord Jesus knows all things, i.e. which actually are, yet if he knows not all future things too, which he himself denies, he falls short of infinite omniscience. For all I know, a finite being may have a knowledge commensurate to this poor earth, which is but "a dust of the balance,"[85] and yet not know all God's secret purposes or the seasons which the Father keeps in his own hand.[86]

---

[84] "Now we know that you know all things, and do not need to have anyone question you; by this we believe that you came from God." John 16:30.

[85] "Behold, the nations are as a drop of a bucket, and are counted as the small dust of the balance: behold, he taketh up the isles as a very little thing." Isaiah 40:15 (KJV).

[86] Acts 1:7.

CHAPTER 3: ANSWERING OBJECTIONS

For another thing, it's objected that the knowledge of the heart is ascribed to Christ.[87] And this, they say, is what belongs to God alone, as Solomon judges,[88] and God claims it as his eminent glory.[89] Yet Jesus Christ says, " I am he who searches the heart."[90] Therefore, they say, surely he must be that God "who only knows the hearts of all the children of men."[91] I take this to be the strongest instance that can be produced from the sacred text for proving that any infinite divine perfections belong to the Lord Jesus Christ, and it shall be seriously considered.

In answer to this, I shall show two things: first, in what sense searching and knowing the heart is made unique to God and incommunicable to others by those texts, and second, even though it is unique to God in some sense, these acts may, in another sense, be rightly attributed to another and performed by someone who is not the Most High God.

As to the former, although Solomon says "You only, Lord, know the hearts of all men," yet what if I say that it's no

---

[87] John 2:25, Matthew 9:9, but especially Revelation 2:23: "And all the churches will know that I am the one who searches minds and hearts, and I will give to each of you as your works deserve."

[88] "then hear in heaven your dwelling place, forgive, act, and render to all whose hearts you know—according to all their ways, for only you know what is in every human heart." 1 Kings 8:39.

[89] "I the Lord test the mind and search the heart, to give to all according to their ways, according to the fruit of their doings." Jeremiah 17:10.

[90] Revelation 2:23.

[91] 1 Kings 8:39.

CHAPTER 3: ANSWERING OBJECTIONS

wonder that Solomon should not know of any other to whom that excellency was communicated, since this mystery of the unsearchable riches and fulness of Christ,[92] and of God's being manifest in his flesh,[93] and his high exaltation of him,[94] was hidden in the ages past and only manifested in the times of the gospel?[95] For it's in these latter times that our Lord Jesus has obtained his great authority and dignity for which he has received appropriate abilities.

Yet I add that such expressions in Scripture appropriating some perfections to God imply only that God has no equal in that respect, or that there is a highest sense only in which such perfections are unique to God and incommunicable to all others, although still in a lower sense something of those perfections may be given by him to others.

---

[92] "the mystery that has been hidden throughout the ages and generations but has now been revealed to his saints. To them God chose to make known how great among the Gentiles are the riches of the glory of this mystery, which is Christ in you, the hope of glory." Colossians 1:26–27.

[93] "And without controversy great is the mystery of godliness: God was manifest in the flesh, justified in the Spirit, seen of angels, preached unto the Gentiles, believed on in the world, received up into glory." 1 Timothy 3:16 (KJV). Emyln evidently understands the first claim here to be that God was manifested *in Jesus'* flesh. Modern translations, which are based on a more accurate Greek text say "He [i.e. Christ] was manifest in the flesh." That the "he" referred to is Jesus, not God, is shown by the final clause, that he was taken up into glory—a reference to Jesus' post-resurrection ascension. (Acts 1:9–11)

[94] Luke 22:69; Acts 2:33; Acts 5:31; Philippians 2:9; Ephesians 1:20; 1 Peter 3:22; Revelation 5:12.

[95] Hebrews 1:1–2.

CHAPTER 3: ANSWERING OBJECTIONS

And this shall be seen in a multitude of instances to be no implausible hypothesis, but rather in accordance with common and clear scriptural statements. Thus, it's said that only God is wise,[96] that only God has immortality,[97] and that only God is holy.[98] Yet there are wise and holy human beings, and immortal holy angels and spirits. But the meaning of those appropriate expressions is that the blessed God is wise and holy and immortal in a more excellent way and in a higher sense than all others—a sense in which others *can't* be wise, holy, and immortal.

So when it's said that God knows the hearts of human beings it must be interpreted the same way, namely, that no one else can know the heart as God does, so universally, so immediately and independently. And yet, it's no contradiction to say that he enables another to do it in a great measure under him. Just as it would be a very weak argument

---

[96] "to the only wise God, through Jesus Christ, to whom be the glory forever! Amen." Romans 16:27. The NRSV translators add a footnote: "Other ancient authorities lack 'to whom.' The verse then reads, 'to the only wise God be the glory through Jesus Christ forever. Amen.'" Emyln here also cites 1 Timothy 1:17, "Now unto the King eternal, immortal, invisible, the only wise God, be honour and glory for ever and ever. Amen." (KJV) Newer translations, being based on more recent critical editions of the Greek originals, omit "wise."

[97] "It is he alone who has immortality and dwells in unapproachable light, whom no one has ever seen or can see; to him be honor and eternal dominion. Amen." 1 Timothy 6:16.

[98] "Lord, who will not fear and glorify your name? For you alone are holy. All nations will come and worship before you, for your judgments have been revealed." Revelation 15:4.

CHAPTER 3: ANSWERING OBJECTIONS

that an angel is God to point out that this angel is called "holy" and "wise," etc., which are said to belong to God only—it would also be a very weak argument that Jesus Christ is the supreme God to point out that he knows the hearts of human beings,[99] which is said to belong to God only[100]—unless they can show that Jesus Christ knows in that same excellent, independent manner and degree as his Father, and that he is no more beholden to the Father for ability and assistance than the Father is to his Son Jesus Christ. Similarly, I might argue from Isaiah that only God knows future events,[101] and yet how often have the prophets foretold them by his inspiration?

It makes sense that holiness and wisdom sufficient for knowing the thoughts and hearts of human beings have been communicated to prophets and apostles. Was there not something of this, if not in the case of the prophet Elisha's telling the secret counsels of the Syrian king,[102] yet at least in the case of the spirit of discerning mentioned by Paul,[103] and in the case of Ananias and Sapphira?[104] I grant this was by divine assistance of the Spirit of God and by revelation.

---

[99] Mark 2:8; Luke 6:8; John 2:25.

[100] 1 Kings 8:39.

[101] "remember the former things of old; for I am God, and there is no other; I am God, and there is no one like me, declaring the end from the beginning and from ancient times things not yet done, saying, 'My purpose shall stand, and I will fulfil my intention.'" Isaiah 46:9–10.

[102] 2 Kings 6:8–12.

[103] 1 Corinthians 12:10.

[104] Acts 5:1–11.

CHAPTER 3: ANSWERING OBJECTIONS

Neither is our Lord Jesus Christ ashamed to admit that his knowledge is sometimes owing to revelation from God his Father. If any should ask how Jesus Christ comes to know all that he reveals in those seven letters to the seven churches,[105] the very first words of that book Revelation may be an answer: it was the revelation which God gave to Jesus Christ.[106] No wonder, then, that he says he knows their works, their hearts, and their approaching judgments and trials, when his own vast abilities are assisted by God's revelation.

But it will be said that his "searching the heart" implies it to be his own act. Answer: so it may very well be, for whatever a human knows, they know it by their own act. And why may not the mind search and yet be under the light of revelation and the influence of superior assistance? Ultimately, these words "searching the heart" are only an expression that denotes the accuracy of his knowledge, not the manner of attaining to it, for taken properly, as applied to God, it's dishonorable to say that God searches for things, since all things are naked and open to his view. And if they must be taken strictly and properly, as applied to Christ, then they don't belong to him in the same sense as they do to God, and so can be no argument for his being that God.

---

[105] Revelation 2–3.
[106] "The revelation of Jesus Christ, which God gave him to show his servants what must soon take place; he made it known by sending his angel to his servant John, who testified to the word of God and to the testimony of Jesus Christ, even to all that he saw." Revelation 1:1–2.

CHAPTER 3: ANSWERING OBJECTIONS

Further, there's no absurdity in attributing *this* knowledge of the heart to Jesus Christ, even though he is not the Most High God. That he knows things with some limitation as to the degree, and in dependence on his Father as to the manner, is clear from what has been said already. Therefore, the knowledge of human hearts that is attributed to him must be such as is consistent with his subordination to the Father's greater knowledge.

One may object: it's impossible for a *finite* being to have such universal knowledge of the hearts and ways of human beings as is ascribed to Jesus Christ and which as the head and ruler of the church and world he ought to have, and therefore he is infinite God.

Answer: I'm pretty sure it can never be proven that it exceeds a finite capacity to know the concerns of all on this earth, when an enlarged understanding is assisted in the highest manner by divine influence and revelation, because the object of this knowledge would be finite. I challenge anyone to show me how it can be impossible for a finite capacity to comprehend a finite object, as this world is, and would be, though it were ten thousand times greater than it is! I am convinced that this can never be shown to imply any contradiction, and that all such imaginations concerning it proceed mainly from too high a view of human beings and too low a view of the infinite God, as if the difference between these were so small that there could not be one made with a mental capacity so much above other humans that his alone equaled all of theirs put together, as if the supreme being

CHAPTER 3: ANSWERING OBJECTIONS

couldn't produce a creature who should be a thousand times greater than all this earth and its inhabitants but still be infinitely below himself. I suppose that if the sun were an intelligent creature who could diffuse his intellectual influences as he does his beams of light and could also see and understand with his beams and secret influences, it's easy to imagine what a penetrating and comprehensive knowledge he might have. But we may entertain much greater thoughts of the Sun of Righteousness, Jesus Christ.[107]

I think that a strong argument to prove that Jesus Christ, as man, is capable of such deep and extensive knowledge may be drawn from the offices of dignity and power conferred on him by God. For God has given to him to be head over all things.[108] He has given or committed to him all judgement,[109] and this *as* the Son of Man.[110] In short, his kingly office, by which he rules over all the world and takes special care of all his members, as it necessarily presupposes his knowledge of the whole condition of his church and every member of it as far as it is necessary for the carrying out of that mission, so I think it undeniably proves this large knowledge to be exercised by him *as man*, however he gains it.

---

[107] Malachi 4:2.

[108] "And he has put all things under his feet and has made him the head over all things for the church." Ephesians 1:22.

[109] "The Father judges no one but has given all judgment to the Son," John 5:22.

[110] "and he has given him authority to execute judgment, because he is the Son of Man." John 5:27.

CHAPTER 3: ANSWERING OBJECTIONS

For since this position and power are given, they cannot be grounded in Christ's divine nature, for who can give to God any dignity or power, since God has all dignity and power originally in his own being? These must then be given to the man or human nature only. And if the *man* Christ Jesus carries out this kingly role and is invested with this kingly power, even with all power in heaven and earth,[111] then *as man* we cannot deny him to be suitably qualified for it with all requisite abilities, lest we criticize God for calling one to a job who is not fitted for it or we criticize Jesus for accepting a mission which he is not able to accomplish. Besides, unless his human nature can execute this power, it cannot be said to be given to it, for a power which can't be exerted or is impossible to exercise is neither given nor received, any more than a commission or grant to a stump or a tree to rule, not over the other trees (as in Jotham's parable),[112] but over a nation, or to command an army. It's no gift at all, if this were the case, that the man Christ Jesus were utterly incapable of the role and government vested in him.

If it be said that although the kingly role and delegated authority is committed to the human nature but is only carried out by the divine nature in Christ, I answer that it's most unreasonable to suppose that this trust is committed to the man Christ, who must finally hand it over,[113] and yet the

---

[111] "And Jesus came and said to them, 'All authority in heaven and on earth has been given to me.'" Matthew 28:18.

[112] Judges 9:1–21.

[113] "Then comes the end, when he hands over the kingdom to God the

CHAPTER 3: ANSWERING OBJECTIONS

management of it belongs only to another being. How can he be commended for being faithful over the house of God, to him who appointed him,[114] when it's not expected he should carry out his function?

I grant, indeed, that his kingly reign is carried out by the assistance of God, as he exerts his divine power and wisdom through the human nature of Christ and gives them in all fulness to him in whom they dwell.[115] But to say that the man Christ does not exercise his kingly, universal power, but that his divine nature (supposing he has such) does solely and immediately execute the office given to him as man or mediator (for nothing can be given to God) is, in my mind, a huge absurdity. For it's to say that God rules over human beings in carrying out a delegated or subordinate authority, or that he acts under the authority and in the name of a creature, which is not properly said of the supreme God. It remains, therefore, that as Christ's universal kingdom and leadership are a gift from God (of which only the man Christ is the

---

Father, after he has destroyed every ruler and every authority and power." 1 Corinthians 15:24.

[114] "Therefore, brothers and sisters, holy partners in a heavenly calling, consider that Jesus, the apostle and high priest of our confession, was faithful to the one who appointed him, just as Moses also 'was faithful in all God's house.' [Numbers 12:7] . . . Now Moses was faithful in all God's house as a servant, to testify to the things that would be spoken later. Christ, however, was faithful over God's house as a son, and we are his house if we hold firm the confidence and the pride that belong to hope." Hebrews 3:1–2, 5–6.

[115] "For in him the whole fullness of deity dwells bodily." Colossians 2:9.

CHAPTER 3: ANSWERING OBJECTIONS

receiver, committed as a mission to him), so he certainly lacks no ability to carry out that mission in the nature entrusted with it—I say, no ability, whether of power or knowledge, sufficient to render him a careful, vigorous, and in every way most effective head of his body and ruler of the world.[116] To deny this is to rob him of his greatest glory.

Besides, what benefit or gift is it to the man Christ that the divine nature should execute a power which it always had and could exercise without any gift to him? What reward or addition would this be to him?

Another argument may be drawn from the comfortable ground of confidence in a Christian's prayers to God which the Scriptures lay down, namely, the sympathizing compassion of our Lord Jesus Christ towards his distressed servants arising from his own sufferings when on earth:

> For we do not have a high priest who is unable to sympathize with our weaknesses, but we have one who in every respect has been tested as we are, yet without sin. Let us therefore approach the throne of grace with boldness.[117]

Christ's having been tried with sufferings makes him a more compassionate and earnest advocate for us, and this is our comfort.

Now it's certain that this compassion arising from his own experience of trouble can belong to none but his human

---

[116] 1 Corinthians 12:12-31.
[117] Hebrews 4:15-16a.

CHAPTER 3: ANSWERING OBJECTIONS

nature. The divine nature is compassionate, but not because it was tempted or grieved with misery. No, it was only the man Christ who suffered and consequently feels a sympathy from this with his distressed servants. And it's most certain that if he sympathizes with them in their troubles, he must then know them in that nature which only has a fellow-feeling with them. For none can sympathize with the miseries of others which he knows nothing about. So that they who deny that Christ's human nature is capable of knowing all our miseries in effect deny him to be such a compassionate advocate as the Scriptures represent him, and rob us of this strong ground of consolation and hope in our approaches to God which the author of Hebrews would have us to build on.

And this doctrine has been so far from appearing either impossible or absurd to the reason of humankind, that I might produce the consent of a very great number of learned men, even among those who oppose my other opinions. The Lutherans allow the man Christ a sort of universal knowledge, as well as universal presence, which they argue for.[118] The Catholic theologians, both Thomists and Scotists, allow him universal knowledge, though they differ in their way of explaining it.[119]

---

[118] That is, some Lutheran theologians assert that Christ, as man, is both omniscient and omnipresent, theorizing that Christ's divine nature somehow gives these divine properties to the human nature. For a clear exposition of such a theory as propounded by Johannes Brenz (1499–1570), see Cross, *Communicatio Idiomatum*, chapter 2.

[119] These Catholic theologians are followers, respectively, of the ideas of

CHAPTER 3: ANSWERING OBJECTIONS

And there was a time in the sixth century when in the Christian church some were branded with the label "heresy" under the name of "Agnoetae," who held that Christ was ignorant of some things, which I suppose must have been in relation to his human nature. For those persons believed him to have a divine nature, and it's hard to imagine they could attribute ignorance to that.[120] But (to leave aside that matter, which is disputed), it is enough for my purpose, namely, to prove what sense the Christian church then had of Christ's extensive knowledge *as man*, that those who wrote against those "heretics" explicitly deny any ignorance in Christ *as man*. For this we may produce two famous patriarchs of the

---

philosopher-theologians Thomas Aquinas (1225–74) and John Duns Scotus (c. 1265–1308). Aquinas argued that because of its union with the Word (the second divine Person of the Trinity) the human soul of Christ must know at least the truths about all past, present, and future events, but not all truths whatever (e.g. some about merely possible events), and so while that soul "knew all things," it was less than omniscient. On this see Aquinas, *Summa Theologica*, 768 (III, Q10, A2) and Adams, *What Sort*, 52–57. For the extremely complicated views of Scotus on the knowledge of Christ's human soul, see Adams, *What Sort*, 78–85.

[120] Monophysite Christians rejected the two-nature Christology of the Council of Chalcedon, insisting instead that after the Incarnation Christ had only one nature, a divine one. Alexandrian deacon Themistius Calonymus, via a now lost controversial writing (c. 534), started a faction among them based on such passages as Mark 13:32, John 11:34, and Luke 2:52, by agreeing with them that Christ's knowledge was limited. As Monophysites, they did believe in such a thing as Christ's humanity, but were opposed to calling it a "nature," and they would have located his limited knowledge there. On this see Grillmeier and Hainthaler, *Christ*, 362–66.

Christian church at that time, Eulogius of Alexandria[121] and Gregory of Rome.[122] Those "heretics" produced as evidence for their opinion Christ's words that he knew not the time of the last judgment, as an instance of his ignorance. To this Eulogius says that he was not ignorant of it as man and much less was he ignorant of it as God. Gregory says, *In natura quidem humanitatis novisse, sed non ex natura humanitatis*. That is, "he knew it with the human nature, but that knowledge did not arise from the humanity,"[123] which is what I maintain as to the knowledge I attribute to him, but not extending it so far as all future events, which they did.

And I find some of the modern Protestant theologians who (when outside of this dispute) speak agreeably to this, and are far from thinking it idolatry to ascribe as much knowledge as I have to the man Christ. Thus, the reverend Mr.

---

[121] Bishop of Alexandria (d. 608 CE).

[122] Pope Gregory I, a.k.a. Saint Gregory the Great (d. 604 CE), remembered particularly for sending missionaries to the British Isles.

[123] In his letter to Eulogius, Gregory first repeats an answer endorsed by the influential North African bishop and theologian Augustine of Hippo (354–430 CE), that "the Almighty Son says He does not know the day ... not because he himself does not know it, but because he does not permit it to be known at all." Gregory I, *Letter*, 311. But then he ventures a second, "more subtle" answer: "that the only-begotten, incarnate and made perfect man for us, did indeed *in* his human nature know the day and the hour of the judgment, but nevertheless did not know this *from* his human nature. What he knew *in* it he did not on that account know *from* it, because God-made-man knew the day and the hour of the judgment by the power of his godhead." Gregory I, *Letter*, 311–12.

CHAPTER 3: ANSWERING OBJECTIONS

Baxter,[124] in his notes on Ephesians 4:16[125] plainly implies that he thinks an angel might be made capable of ruling the universal church on earth by legislation, judgment, and governance. For having said that such descriptions wouldn't be apt to any power but divine, he corrects himself by adding "or angelical at least,"[126] and surely the man Christ's ability is far superior to angels, for he has them ministering to him and giving him reports of matters if there be any occasion, for he has seven principal spirits who are the "eyes of the Lamb sent forth through all the earth," as the same author interprets Revelation 5:6.

Again, the author of the little book called *The Future State*,[127] the same who wrote the *Good Samaritan*, a worthy clergyman of the Church of England, says many reasonable things about the large extent of Christ's human knowledge, such as that probably "he can as easily inspect the whole globe of the earth and the heavens that surround it as we can view a

---

[124] English Puritan theologian Richard Baxter (1615–91).

[125] "But speaking the truth in love, we must grow up in every way into him who is the head, into Christ, from whom the whole body, joined and knit together by every ligament with which it is equipped, as each part is working properly, promotes the body's growth in building itself up in love." Ephesians 4:15–16.

[126] Baxter, *A Paraphrase*, note on Ephesians 4:16.

[127] *The Future State* has been attributed to George Jones or Edward Whitaker, or both. In 1640 an Anglican minister named Nehemiah Rodgers (1593–1660) published a book titled *The Good Samaritan*. It is not clear if Emlyn had this work in mind or another of the same title, or if he has mistaken the author's identity.

CHAPTER 3: ANSWERING OBJECTIONS

globe of an inch diameter."[128] "That he intercedes as man. And can he intercede in a case which he doesn't know?"[129] Limborch[130] says much the same in his *Institutes of Christian Theology,* book 5, chapter 18.[131]

Let me add the testimony of Dr. Thomas Goodwin,[132] who was never, I suppose, criticized for being an idolater among the Dissenters.[133] Yet it's hardly possible that I should attribute greater knowledge to the man Jesus Christ than he

---

[128] *The Future State*, 46–47.

[129] *The Future State*, 150.

[130] Dutch Arminian theologian Philipp van Limborch (1633–1712).

[131] Limborch is answering those who would object to worshipping Christ not as God but as man or as mediator: "Thirdly, they object, 'Cursed is the man who trusts in man.' (Jeremiah 17:5) But Jesus Christ as mediator was *man*. Answer: What does this text have to do with the honor paid to Christ as mediator? In this text, people are rebuked who put their confidence merely in human assistance; 'man' therefore signifies frail and mortal man, as appears by what immediately follows, 'and makes flesh his arm,' that is, who trusts in the strength of men, who are merely perishable flesh. Such people indeed cast away their confidence in God, rely upon weak humanity, and therefore are threatened with a severe punishment. But our Lord Jesus Christ, who has been exalted into heaven, is not flesh but rather a quickening spirit, having dominion over all things, and is endowed by God the Father with omniscience and with power. Therefore, one who trusts in him does not rely on flesh, nor do they cast away their confidence in God, but they thereby obey and depend upon God alone." Limborch, *Compleat System*, 543 (5.8.2), modernized; see also the original Latin: Limborch, *Institutiones,* 473 (5.18.12).

[132] Thomas Goodwin (1600–80), English Puritan theologian and president of Magdalen College of Oxford University.

[133] This term refers to Protestants in the 1600s and 1700s who were not a part of the Church of England (i.e. not Anglicans).

CHAPTER 3: ANSWERING OBJECTIONS

does where he says that the human understanding of Christ takes in all occurrences which concern his church, and since Christ said, "All power in heaven and earth is given to me by my Father,"[134] he might as well say that "all knowledge in heaven and earth is given me," that his vision pierces into every corner, that he knows the grief in every heart. He concludes with this remarkable thought, that as a spherical mirror represents the images of all that is in the room, so the enlarged human understanding of Christ takes in all things in heaven and earth at once.[135] It seems these men did *not* take it to be the

---

[134] Matthew 28:18.

[135] Emlyn paraphrases Goodwin here. A slightly modernized and fuller quotation from the passage is: "Now, therefore, to explicate the way how our miseries are let into [Christ's] heart and come to stir up such kindly affections of pity and compassion in him. . . . The understanding and knowledge of that human nature has notice and cognizance of all the occurrences that befall his members here. And for this the text [Hebrews 2:14–18] is clear, for the apostle speaks this for our encouragement, that Christ is touched with the feeling of our infirmities—which could not be a relief to us unless it implied that he particularly and distinctly knew them, for if he knew some but not all, we should lack relief in all because we would not know which he knew and which he did not. And the apostle affirms this of his human nature . . . for he speaks of that nature which was tempted here below. And, therefore, the Lamb that was slain, and so the man Christ Jesus, is said to have 'seven eyes' as well as 'seven horns,' which seven eyes are 'the seven spirits sent forth into all the earth.' (Revelation 5:6) His eyes of providence, through his anointing with the Holy Spirit, are in all corners of the world, and view all the things that are done under the sun. In like manner he is there said to have seven horns for power, as seven eyes for knowledge, and both are defined to be seven, to show the perfection of both in their extent (reaching unto all things) so that, as all power in heaven and earth is committed unto him, as Son of man, as the

unique perfection of the divine nature to know our hearts, so no creature could partake of it by divine assistance and revelation.

Indeed, as to the manner of knowing human hearts, we cannot tell how the inhabitants of the other world have access to our minds or to each other's. But without a doubt, Jesus Christ, whose eyes are as a flame of fire,[136] has more penetrating vision, as well as more revelation from God and more capacity for receiving and treasuring it up, than all others.

In short, it's clear that Christ *as man* is the great administrator of God's providential kingdom. As man he must judge the whole world, which implies vast and universal knowledge.[137] Who then should dare to say that the *man* Christ Jesus lacks a knowledge which is, without exaggeration, as large as this narrow earth or as multitudinous as the sand by the seashore? I think it's beyond all reasonable doubt. And as

---

Scripture speaks, so all knowledge is given him of all things done heaven and earth, and this as Son of Man too: his knowledge and power being of equal extent. He is the sun, as well in respect of knowledge as of righteousness, and there is nothing hid from his sight and beams, which pierce the darkest corners of the hearts of the sons of men. He knows the griefs . . . and distresses of their hearts. Just as a looking-glass made into the form of a round globe and hung in the middle of a room takes in all the images of things done or that are therein at once, so does the enlarged understanding of Christ's human nature take in the affairs of this world which he is appointed to govern, especially the miseries of his members, and this at once." Goodwin, *The Heart*, 309–10, modernized.

[136] Revelation 1:14; Revelation 19:12.
[137] John 5:27; Acts 17:31.

CHAPTER 3: ANSWERING OBJECTIONS

this doctrine has appeared rational enough and has escaped all condemnation when stated by non-unitarians, so I hope this view will not be counted "heretical" when held by unitarians, as the non-unitarians never had to forfeit the glorious title of "orthodox" on account of this doctrine.

Thus it appears that all that's said of Christ's extensive knowledge in Scripture is far from proving him to be the supreme, infinite God; it is well explained in other ways. And the same is true for features attributed to him which some call "divine perfections." These are no more truly infinite when attributed to him than is this knowledge just discussed. There are clear evidences of their being attributed to him in a limited and inferior sense in comparison with what they are in the most glorious "God over all gods."[138] Therefore, there will need to be other arguments if the supreme deity of Christ is going to be established.

---

[138] "For you, O LORD, are most high over all the earth; you are exalted far above all gods." Psalm 97:9; "For I know that the LORD is great; our Lord is above all gods." Psalm 135:5; "O give thanks to the LORD, for he is good, for his steadfast love endures forever. O give thanks to the God of gods, for his steadfast love endures forever." Psalm 136:1–2. The word "gods" in these passages is being used not for a true peer of God, an impossibility, but rather for unseen, powerful beings generally, of which God is the greatest.

CHAPTER 3: ANSWERING OBJECTIONS

3.2 *Answering Arguments from the Worship of Jesus*

No doubt I could maintain my cause just as well on the topic of divine worship, which is another way my opposers would try to establish the deity of the Lord Jesus Christ. But it's easy to show that there is no instance of supreme, divine worship given ultimately to Christ in Scripture, but on the contrary, all the honor it assigns to him is such as assumes him to be inferior to the Father and dependent on him, since it is wholly grounded upon what God his Father has graciously bestowed on him.

Thus, he requires baptism (if that's an act of immediate, proper worship) in his name because "all power in heaven and earth" was given to him.[139] Thus, we must honor the Son as truly as (not as greatly as) we honor the Father, because the Father has committed, or given, all judgment to him.[140] Thus, at "the name of Jesus every knee must bow, and every tongue confess him to be Lord," because as a reward for his obedience,

---

[139] "And Jesus came and said to them, 'All authority in heaven and on earth has been given to me. Go therefore and make disciples of all nations, baptizing them in the name of the Father and of the Son and of the Holy Spirit, and teaching them to obey everything that I have commanded you. And remember, I am with you always, to the end of the age.' " Matthew 28:18–20.

[140] "The Father judges no one but has given all judgment to the Son, so that all may honor the Son just as they honor the Father. Anyone who does not honor the Son does not honor the Father who sent him." John 5:22–23.

CHAPTER 3: ANSWERING OBJECTIONS

the Father "has given him a name above every name." And it's added that all this honor is ultimately to the "glory of the Father."[141]

Worship which is thus grounded upon derived and borrowed excellence is not *supremely* divine, and cannot be offered to the infinite, self-existent, independent deity without a great offense, because it's not the most excellent.[142] To praise an *independent* God for honor and power granted to him by another presupposes a falsehood and mixes together belittlements with praise.

Although there may be the same common, external acts or words (such as bowing the knee, and saying "glory and praise," etc.) directed to both God and to the mediator, as also in some instances they are given to ordinary people, yet the mind of a rational worshiper will make a distinction in his inward intention, as no doubt those devout Jews did, who in the same act "bowed their heads, and worshiped both God and the King."[143] But I shall not pursue this any further now.[144]

---

[141] "he humbled himself and became obedient to the point of death—even death on a cross. Therefore God also highly exalted him and gave him the name that is above every name, so that at the name of Jesus every knee should bend, in heaven and on earth and under the earth, and every tongue should confess that Jesus Christ is Lord, to the glory of God the Father." Philippians 2:8–11.

[142] "Cursed be the cheat who has a male in the flock and vows to give it, and yet sacrifices to the Lord what is blemished; for I am a great King, says the Lord of hosts, and my name is reverenced among the nations." Malachi 1:14.

[143] 1 Chronicles 29:20.

[144] Emlyn says more about supreme vs. inferior worship in his *A*

CHAPTER 3: ANSWERING OBJECTIONS

Moreover, I judge that to assert Jesus Christ to be the supreme God destroys the gospel-doctrine of his mediation.[145] For if I must have one who is both supreme God and man to be my mediator with God, then when I speak to Jesus Christ as the supreme God, where is the godman that must be my mediator with him? To say he mediates for himself is the same as to say that I must go to him *without* a mediator, and turns the whole business of mediation into a metaphor, contrary both to the common way of things, and to the Scriptures. And I would like to know what is this idea of going to God without a mediator, if it is just that he mediates for himself? Who ever doubted the exercise of his own wisdom or mercy, that these, in a manner of speaking, argue within him? But undeniably the Scriptures speak of a mediator *outside* of God when they set forth Jesus Christ as such.

And who could this mediator be, if (as alleged) we go to Jesus Christ as the *ultimate* object of our supplication? If one says that only his human nature mediates, though as united to his divine nature, I object that this is still to make Christ the mediator for himself, for the human nature is not a godman, and if the man or human nature alone is capable of being a mediator, then it's not necessary that Jesus Christ should be more than a man inhabited by and related to God, in order to be able to play that role. Nor may it be said that its union with the divine nature gives an infinite efficacy to those acts of

---

Vindication and his *An Answer*.
[145] 1 Timothy 2:5.

CHAPTER 3: ANSWERING OBJECTIONS

which the human nature alone is the source. For unless by that union the human nature was turned into an infinite or divine nature, its acts can no more be considered properly and intrinsically infinite in this case than his body or human understanding are infinite because they are united to an infinite, divine nature.

But what fully proves that the human nature of Christ can never be an effectual mediator, according to them, even though it's personally united to the divine nature, is that they deny this human nature, being so united, to have knowledge of the secret mental prayers, the inward desires and distresses of all Christians, or to know anyone's heart. How then can he be a compassionate intercessor in cases that he knows nothing of? How can he sympathize with their sufferings which he doesn't know that they feel at all? What comfort is there in this understanding of Christ's mediation? The divine nature is precluded from it, because they direct us to address ourselves to that nature as the ultimate object of our supplication through a mediator, and the human nature, they say, can know nothing of our plight, nor does it know our hearts, whether we worship sincerely, or repent sincerely, or merely hypocritically, and so doesn't know how to represent or recommend us to God. What a sorry state do these theologians put us in! There is no mediator left to come between us and the supreme God, so we must deal with him immediately and alone, which they must admit is far from the gospel-doctrine or method. Thus is the Lord Jesus ejected from his role, on a pretense of giving him higher honor!

CHAPTER 3: ANSWERING OBJECTIONS

On the whole, as far as I can see, we're better off being content with the apostle Paul's clear and straightforward account of this matter (if its being so very intelligible doesn't count as an unpardonable objection against it), namely, that "there is but one God, and one mediator between God and men, the man Christ Jesus."[146] Be assured that the apostle Paul knew how to describe the mediator without leaving out the better half of him, or the more important nature. Our mediator, according to him, was only called a "man," although he is also by role a god, a ruler over all, made so by him who puts all things under him.

And indeed, as there are two principal, distinguishing doctrines of Christianity—the unity of the supreme God, and the one mediator between us and him—so the trinitarians have lost them both among their various factions. For as they are divided into two main factions (besides several subdivisions), both among Conformists and Dissenters,[147] one group holding *three* real persons (or infinite beings), the other only *one* (for they are not yet agreed whether they worship three infinite, supreme beings or only one), so between them both, these two great doctrines are undermined.[148] The "Realists," those who think the

---

[146] 1 Timothy 2:5 (KJV).

[147] That is, Anglicans and non-Anglican Protestants.

[148] Here Emlyn shows that he's read some of the controversial literature on "the Trinity" from the 1690s. One unitarian tract pointed out that some trinitarians think the "Persons" of the Trinity as three selves or intelligent agents, whereas others reduce these "Persons" to ways the one

CHAPTER 3: ANSWERING OBJECTIONS

"Persons" of the Trinity are persons, leave room for a mediator in the Trinity, but they destroy the unity of God, who is *one* infinite being. On the other hand, they who hold true to the divine unity, believing in one infinite being with three modes or properties or relations, do by clear implication leave no place for such a mediator as they would like to have, namely, one who is an infinite God, to be a mediator *with* the infinite God, when there is no *other* infinite being but him. Nor can he be thought to intercede with himself. To keep the gospel-faith whole and undefiled it's necessary to sail between both of these rocks by believing God and his Christ to be two beings, so in this way there will be room for one to mediate for the other, and these two will not be two equal supreme beings, but rather one will be subordinate to the other, so in this way we may preserve the unity of the supreme God.

Therefore, let us seriously consider not what the church in these latter days has thought about Jesus Christ, but rather what his own apostles, when inspired, have thought about him. I think no one was more likely, or ever had a better opportunity to describe his Lord in the height of his glory than the apostle Peter on the day of Pentecost, that day of triumph, with the newly and visibly inspired apostles. Hear

---

divine self is. The tract calls the former "Real" trinitarians and the latter "Nominal" trinitarians. (Dixon, *Nice and Hot*, 131–32; Nye, *Discourse*) Trinitarians who dare to interpret the traditional language can still, for the most part, be divided into those who think the "Persons" of the Trinity to be three selves and those who think they involve only one. On this see Tuggy, "Trinity," sections 1–2.

CHAPTER 3: ANSWERING OBJECTIONS

how magnificently he describes his glorious Lord Jesus in front of his murderers: "You men of Israel hear these words. Jesus of Nazareth, a man approved by God among you by miracles, wonders, and signs which God did by him in your midst."[149] Again, "Let all the house of Israel know assuredly that God has made that same Jesus whom you have crucified both Lord and Christ."[150] We observe that the apostle was aiming at such a description of Christ as might strike the hearts of his murderers with the greatest horror about their crime, and therefore he could never omit the most impressive portion of his description, namely Christ's infinite deity, if he had really been such. What a terrifying argument that would have been, able to produce more conviction in his persecutors than all the rest, to tell them that they had shed the blood of the infinite God himself. What the apostle Peter says is certainly dull and weak in comparison with this, namely that he was a man approved by God. Did he not understand his mission, or was he trying to thwart it by such an omission? And yet, when he was far from being held back by any fear to confess Christ fully, he only describes Christ as a god by inhabitation and exaltation. Furthermore, if the deity of Christ were a fundamental teaching of the Christian faith, why is it that when poor, convicted souls, in anguish for their crimes, seek advice about how to be saved from them,[151] the apostle should not acquaint them with this teaching, but

---

[149] Acts 2:22.
[150] Acts 2:36.
[151] Acts 2:37.

instead directs them to believe in Jesus as described above? Did he direct wounded souls to an insufficient savior by not telling them that he was the infinite God? Yet they are baptized and added to the church and numbered among such as shall be saved.[152] How can this be, if the supreme deity of Christ is a fundamental teaching of the Christian faith? Likewise, he later preaches that "God was with him."[153] This was all.

3.3 *Protestants' Anti-Catholic Arguments Re-applied to Themselves*

To conclude, God and Christ (i.e. one anointed) are two separate or different beings as much as Christ's body and the communion bread are, and therefore many correct descriptions of one can't also be applied to the other in a proper or literal sense, as all our writers against the Catholic

---

[152] Acts 2:41.

[153] "Then Peter began to speak to them: 'I truly understand that God shows no partiality, but in every nation anyone who fears him and does what is right is acceptable to him. You know the message he sent to the people of Israel, preaching peace by Jesus Christ—he is Lord of all. That message spread throughout Judea, beginning in Galilee after the baptism that John announced: how God anointed Jesus of Nazareth with the Holy Spirit and with power; how he went about doing good and healing all who were oppressed by the devil, for God was with him.'" Acts 10:34–38.

CHAPTER 3: ANSWERING OBJECTIONS

doctrine of transubstantiation argue, and it's of equal force in the present case.[154]

To be anointed implies having been raised up by an authority and having honor conferred upon one. It's in effect to say that the person is a creature, an inferior being. Therefore, to say that actually Christ is the most high God is to say the inferior is supreme, and the man is God, which cannot be true, except understood non-literally, as for example the bread "is" Christ's body, namely by being in some way related to it, etc. And truly, if the issue can be fixed here by making a personal union between God and Christ, I don't

---

[154] Early modern Protestant writers often used the Roman Catholic doctrine of transubstantiation as an example of a doctrine which Christians can't reasonably believe. According to this doctrine, based on a literal reading of passages such as Mark 14:22–25 and John 6:53–55, and formulated (or some would argue refined) in the high middle ages, when the priest in the Mass blesses the bread and the wine, their substances (underlying realities) turn, respectively, into the substance of Jesus' body and the substance of Jesus' blood, while their "accidents" (i.e. observable, non-essential features, such as weight, color, and taste) remain the same. This doctrine implies that when one eats and drinks (what appear to be) the bread and wine, one is actually consuming the entire body and blood of Jesus. Protestants object that our God-given senses (sight, touch, smell, taste) are telling us that the objects before us are merely a small, circular wafer and a portion of wine in a cup, not a man's whole body and all of a man's blood. It looks like we have more evidence that the items before us are mere bread and wine than we do to accept the Catholic teaching of transubstantiation. In response one famous Catholic writer doubled down, urging that "If we wish to proceed securely in all things, we must hold fast to the following principle: What seems to me white, I will believe black if the hierarchical Church so defines." Loyola, *The Spiritual Exercises*, 365.

CHAPTER 3: ANSWERING OBJECTIONS

see why a Catholic can't set up another such "union" between Christ's body and the bread in the eucharist, and then they may stoutly defend the claim that it's really the body of Christ.

But indeed nothing is more obvious than the unsteadiness of many Protestant writers when they write against the Catholics and then against the unitarians. How do they go both backwards and forwards? And when they have triumphantly and fully defeated the ineffective attacks and objections of the Catholics, they take up the Catholics' refuted arguments and redeploy them against the unitarians. And what they have maintained against the Catholics as good arguments (notwithstanding Catholic evasions), these same arguments they oppose when the unitarians turn them against themselves on the topic of the Trinity. These Protestant writers themselves resort to similar tricks and evasions as the Catholics.

Thus, when the Catholics object to the novelty of the Protestant religion and ask them where were their religion and church before Luther, the Protestants think this is a weak quibble, and can tell them their religion was in the Bible, and their church among the earliest Christians, even though it lay hidden during the centuries of widespread apostacy. And yet to the unitarians they make the same objection: "Where has any Christian church, for so many ages, held that Christ was not God?"

Against the Catholics the Protestants will prove that the ancient "fathers" did not hold the elements to be Christ's real body and blood, because they often call them the "images" of

CHAPTER 3: ANSWERING OBJECTIONS

them. But when the unitarians argue that Christ is not the supreme God because the Scriptures call him "the image of God"—and therefore he is not the God whose image only he is[155]—now, according to these Protestants, the thing itself and its image must be the same thing.

Against the Catholics they prove that the apostle Peter was subject to the church and to the rest of the apostles (though not singly to each) because he was sent here and there by them.[156] This Baronius takes hold of and tells them that by the same reason they must grant the "Arians' " argument to be a good one, namely that the Father is greater than the Son because the Son is sent by him.[157] But when a unitarian argues in this way, now although the Father sends and the Son is sent by him, yet they shall both be equal, and this shall make no difference.

Against the Catholics the Protestants will boast that they don't hoodwink the people in ignorance, but rather they invite them to inquire and examine matters, and the more the better, while it's a ground of suspicion that the Catholics cheat

---

[155] "Of course the image and the one of whom he is the image are not to be thought of as one and the same thing, but as two beings [translators' footnote: *ousiai*], two things, and two powers, corresponding to the number of their names." Eusebius, *Against Marcellus*, 109 (1.41). See also 2 Corinthians 4:4, Colossians 1:15.

[156] Acts 8:14.

[157] Counter-Reformation era Roman Catholic cardinal and church historian Caesar Baronius (1538–1607), presumably in his 12-volume *Annales Ecclesiastici a Christo Nato ad Annum 1198* [*Ecclesiastical Annals from Christ's Nativity to 1198*] (1588–1607).

CHAPTER 3: ANSWERING OBJECTIONS

people by keeping them from the light. But now when it comes to the unitarians, they do a one-eighty and warn people against reading and arguing. They are now for "implicit faith"[158] without examining into deep mysteries; they ask us to believe and not pry into them, though we only desire to examine whether the Scriptures actually reveal any such mysteries at all. The rest we will believe if we could see that. We desire no other freedom in interpreting Scripture than that which they so reasonably help themselves to in interpreting Christ's words, "This is my body."[159] Given Protestant standards, the unitarians think they can stand their ground and defend themselves in these matters as easily as the Protestants can against the Catholics.

As to the earliest Christian times, so many inquirers both among the Catholic and Reformed writers have given their

---

[158] "Implicit faith" is a term much criticized by early modern Protestant writers, though it has fallen out of use by Catholics in more recent times. Thomas Aquinas, realizing that ordinary people basically never think about and probably don't grasp the meaning of a great many Church teachings, suggests that it is enough, at least in the case of secondary teachings, that such people believe *whatever it is* which is taught by Catholic scholars, insofar as it agrees with Scripture. This he calls "implicit faith" with regard to those teachings; put more clearly, such people don't *believe* such teachings, but rather they are "ready to believe them" were they able to think about them. Perhaps surprisingly, given the extreme difficulty of Aquinas's expositions of them, Aquinas is clear that "implicit" faith is not enough when it comes to Church teaching on Incarnation and Trinity. (Aquinas, *Summa*, 390–99, Second Part, Part II, Q2, A1–9.)

[159] Mark 14:22.

impartial testimony that they tended towards Arius's doctrine,[160] and have made such poor excuses for these "fathers," as if they didn't know or were not careful about their fundamental doctrines until these came to be debated in "ecumenical" councils, that I think I needn't say more. I would suggest only one thing: any honest person must grant that the earliest writers speak in different places with great (at least seeming) discord. Sometimes they plainly declare that Jesus Christ was inferior to and the servant of the Father before his incarnation, while at other times they give him high titles which suggest that he is equal with God. Yet it's far more reasonable to suppose that the higher expressions should be explained according to the lower, rather than the contrary, because in discoursing about and pleading for a beloved, admired object, as the Lord Jesus deserves to be, it's very easy and natural to wax eloquent and embark on lofty flights of praise which must be interpreted not with strict rigor, but rather in much lesser ways. This is how we interpret some of the Protestants' lofty tributes to the venerable mystery of the eucharist, as though with the Catholics they took the elements

---

[160] That is, a teaching about God and the Son like that of the Alexandrian presbyter Arius (d. 336 CE), so that the Father alone is the one true God, and the Son (or the Word of John 1) is a second and lesser being who was caused to existed by God (either eternally or a finite time ago). For a full account of Arius's views see Williams, *Arius*, 95–116. For many examples of this sort of subordinationism among theologians of the first three Christian centuries, see Lamson, *The Church*; Tuggy and Date, *Is Jesus*, 65–67, 76–80, 114–15, 123–26, 142–45, 153–56; Tuggy, "The Lost Early History."

CHAPTER 3: ANSWERING OBJECTIONS

to be Christ's real body. But on the contrary, no one is ever inclined to speak diminutively on such occasions; they could not have a thought to lessen their master's glory. Therefore, if the "fathers" ever describe him as *not* the supreme God, nor equal to him, we have all reason to think that they spoke the words of truth and sobriety, and what the exact matter required.

For my own part, I write this while being duly impressed by those great relations in which the blessed Jesus stands to me, whom I credit as my great teacher, whom I desire to admire and love as my gracious, endeared benefactor—beyond father or mother or friends, etc.—whom I revere as my Lord and ruler, and solemnly expect as my final, glorious judge, who is to come in his own and in his Father's glory, and through whom in the meantime I deal with God, as my only mediator and intercessor. Therefore, I earnestly profess that it's not without grievous and bitter displeasure that I should be employed in writing things which by so many well-meaning Christians will be misinterpreted to be derogatory to the honor of this great redeemer. But I know he loves nothing but truth in his cause, and will never be offended, I hope, with any who stand by his own words, namely, "The Father is greater than I."[161] I think it a dangerous thing to say that God is *not* greater than he, or is *not* "the head of Christ,"[162] for "'To whom then will you compare me, or who is my equal?' says

---

[161] John 14:28.
[162] 1 Corinthians 11:3.

the Holy One."[163] I am persuaded that it's truth I plead for and that supports me.

3.4 *Conclusion: A Call for Temperance*

However, I wish they who are adversaries to my position would learn at least the modesty of one of the earliest extant writers for Christianity after the apostles. I mean Justin Martyr, disputing with Trypho the Jew, and arguing for the honor of Jesus Christ, whom he calls "a deity by the will of the Father," and one who "ministered to his will" before his Incarnation.[164] This person attempts to show that Jesus Christ did pre-exist of old, as a "god" (in his sense) and was later born of a virgin. But because, as he says, there were some who confessed him to be Christ and yet denied those points of his pre-existence and his miraculous birth from a virgin, Justin calmly says to his adversary,

> If I shall not demonstrate these things, that he did pre-exist etc., and was born of a virgin, yet still the

---

[163] Isaiah 40:25.

[164] "Christ ministered to the will of the Father, yet he is a deity because he is the first-begotten of all creatures." Justin, *Dialogue*, 125.3, editors' translation. For Justin the existence of the Son depends on God's will. Speaking of how God caused the Son to exist before the Genesis creation, Justin writes that "this power [i.e. the pre-human Son] was generated from the Father, by his power and will." Justin, *Dialogue*, 194 (128.4); see also 195 (129.3), 93–94 (61.1).

CHAPTER 3: ANSWERING OBJECTIONS

cause is not lost, as to his being the Christ of God. If I do not prove that he did pre-exist etc., it is just to say that I'm mistaken about this thing only. It doesn't follow that he is not the Christ. For whoever he is, it is fully proven that he is the Christ.[165]

As for those Christians who denied the aforementioned things and held him to be only a man who was born in the ordinary way, Justin only says of them "with whom I do not agree."[166] He does not damn them who differed from him, nor will he say (in the ranting dialect of some in our age) that the Christian religion is undermined and that Christ is only an impostor and a broken reed to trust in unless he is the truly supreme God. To the contrary, still he was sure that he is the

---

[165] Emlyn paraphrases in his translation here. The whole passage in a recent translation is: "But since it has been proved beyond all doubt that he is the Christ of God, whatever that Christ eventually is to be, even if I fail to show that he pre-existed, and consented to become man with a body and feelings like our own, according to the will of the Father; only in this last regard could you rightly claim that I have been wrong. But you cannot deny that he is the Christ, even though [i.e. even *if*] he apparently is of human origin, and evidently became the Christ by the Father's choice." Justin, *Dialogue*, 73 (48.3).

[166] "For, my friends, there are some of your race [i.e. Jews, although some editors think this passage should be corrected to read "our," i.e. Christians] who acknowledge that he is the Christ, but claim that he has a merely human origin. I naturally disagree with such persons, nor would I agree with them even if the majority of those who share my opinions were to say so. For we have been told by Christ himself not to follow the teachings of men, but only those which have been announced by the holy prophets and taught by himself." Justin, *Dialogue*, 74 (48.4).

true Christ, whatever else he might be mistaken in. It's desperate wickedness to risk the reputation of the genuineness and holiness of the blessed Jesus because of a difficult and disputable opinion, to dare to say that if they are mistaken in their opinion (which I truly believe they are) then Jesus Christ is a liar and a deceiver, a fake savior, and the like. What is this but to expose Jesus to the scorn of unbelievers?

Thus, I see with sorrow that to this very day, even among professed Christians themselves, Christ crucified is to some a stumbling-block, and to others foolishness.[167] But even if he isn't as good and great as the God who appointed him to be a savior, it is still agreed that he's a "man approved by God by signs and wonders which God did through him,"[168] and by whom (as the instrument) God made the worlds,[169] and that

---

[167] 1 Corinthians 1:23.

[168] Acts 2:22.

[169] Emlyn refers here to this famous passage, the opening of the letter to the Hebrews: "Long ago God spoke to our ancestors in many and various ways by the prophets, but in these last days he has spoken to us by a Son, whom he appointed heir of all things, through whom he also created the worlds. He is the reflection of God's glory and the exact imprint of God's very being, and he sustains all things by his powerful word. When he had made purification for sins, he sat down at the right hand of the Majesty on high, having become as much superior to angels as the name he has inherited is more excellent than theirs." (Hebrews 1:1–4) Like the majority, Emlyn thinks the creation mentioned here, of "worlds" or "ages" (Greek: *aionas*), is the one described in Genesis 1, so that God created the cosmos through the pre-human Jesus. Some unitarians Christians agree with Emyln, while others hold that it is Christ's "new creation" of this and the coming ages which is meant. Whichever side is correct, it remains that the Father only is "creator" in the sense of being the *ultimate* source of the

CHAPTER 3: ANSWERING OBJECTIONS

he is granted to be one in whom dwelt (so as it never dwelt before in prophets or any other) all the fulness of the divine nature,[170] and that he is one with the Father by unity of consent and will (as John Calvin[171] interprets John 10:30), one in testimony with the Father and Spirit (as Theodore Beza[172] and many others understand that in 1 John 5:7),[173] and that he is the most lively, visible image of God that the world ever saw, so that he who sees him does in great measure see the Father (as in a bright mirror[174]), and that he is confessed and served as one far above angels and archangels,[175] and over all powers in heaven and earth,[176] a god or ruler, the great administrator of God's kingdom both on earth and in the invisible *hades*, as having the keys (or ministerial power) of death and hell.[177]

---

cosmos. On this text and on the ambiguity of the idea of being involved in creation, see Tuggy and Date, *Is Jesus*, 71, 116–19, 145–48.

[170] Colossians 2:9.

[171] French reformer for whom "Calvinism" is named, 1509–64.

[172] French Reformed theologian and scholar, 1519–1605.

[173] The King James Version which Emlyn knew had this verse as "For there are three that bear record in heaven, the Father, the Word, and the Holy Ghost: and these three are one." But all translations in recent times acknowledge that no ancient Greek manuscript reads this way, so they have something similar to the NRSV for 1 John 5:7: "There are three that testify"—and these are specified in the next verse: "the Spirit and the water and the blood, and these three agree." On this discrepancy between the KJV and more recent translations see Wallace, "The Textual Problem."

[174] John 14:9.

[175] Hebrews 1–2.

[176] Colossians 1:16.

[177] Revelation 1:18.

CHAPTER 3: ANSWERING OBJECTIONS

Yet after all this, if he isn't the very supreme God himself, and moreover, to complete the absurdity, if he isn't the very same God whose Son and image he is, he shall be no mediator in their eyes. They do, on this supposition, openly disown him as their savior and confidence. They are ashamed to trust in him and seem rather to mock and criticize him as insufficient and insignificant than to believe in him.[178] These things are to

---

[178] The editor Sollom Emlyn here adds some examples in contemporary polemical trinitarian sermons: "it will be fitting for us to pity those who make a subordinate, dependent, deficient god and saviour the object of their hope and trust ... But such a god as this is not to be found in all the Scriptures ... We may safely leave it to those who can be content with such a god and consider it worth their while to contend for, trust in, serve, and worship so ignorant, defective, and imperfect a god as a created god must be, even though he had all the glory conferred upon him that he could possibly bear or be capable of. Such a god as this could at best have none but subordinate excellencies and perfections (though I think a subordinate omnipotence and a subordinate omnipotence sound a bit odd). He could be only a subordinate savior and help us to only a subordinate salvation." Calamy, *Thirteen Sermons*, 130, modernized. And, "While looking to an Arian savior may well enough create a chilling damp in our hearts, dispiriting us with fear, lest someone should 'pluck us out of his hands' [John 10:28], fill us with jealousy lest we go astray and be disappointed, and woefully cramp us in confiding in him. Nor can I, I confess, discern how the apostle Paul could, given the new [Arian] scheme, have cried out so freely at one time, 'I know whom I have believed, and I am persuaded that he is able to keep that which I have committed to him against that Day' [2 Timothy 1:12], and at another time, 'I am persuaded that neither death nor life nor angels nor principalities or powers nor things present, nor things to come, nor height, nor depth, nor any other creature, shall be able to separate us from the love of God which is in Christ Jesus our Lord' [Romans 8:38–39], as he might and could and did given the old [trinitarian] scheme." Calamy, *Thirteen Sermons*, 360, modernized.

CHAPTER 3: ANSWERING OBJECTIONS

me a very grievous offence. I think it a great pity that so excellent a constitution as the gospel is, so lovely to contemplate, so fitting to receive our thankful admiration for the grace and wisdom it contains, should either be lost in the clouds of an artificial obscurity, or exposed to the derision of ungodly scoffers.

It's yet another grief to think what a fatal stop is hereby put to the progress of the gospel, whose rejection by Jews, Muslims, and pagans is undeniably motivated by the common doctrine of the Incarnation of God. One may read in le Compte's history of China how the heathens derided the Christians' doctrine of a mortal God,[179] and for that reason considered Christianity as mythical as their own religion. And Dr. Casaubon[180] in his book on credulity and incredulity says that he could prove by many instances out of history that this "doctrine has kept more people from embracing the Christian

---

[179] French author Louis le Comte (1655–1728) writes of a Chinese court scholar who'd been so humiliated by the superior mathematical abilities of some of the Catholic missionaries that he wanted to persuade the court "that the Christian religion contained much greater errors than those he was guilty of. In the midst of some meetings where the Emperor was present he behaved in such a manner as the Emperor could scarcely bear with him. He laid his hands across and cried out as loud as he could, 'See here, and look what these fellows adore, and what they would have us worship too: a man who was hanged, a person who was crucified! Let anyone judge hereby of their understanding and good sense!' " le Comte, *Memoirs*, 364, modernized.

[180] French-English classical scholar Meric Casaubon (1599–1671).

CHAPTER 3: ANSWERING OBJECTIONS

faith than any other thing" he knew of.[181] Now though I grant that if it be the certain truth of God, this must be no argument against receiving it, yet surely it should make us very cautious and impartial in our inquiry about it, lest we bring on ourselves the woe denounced against them by whom offenses (that is, stumbling-blocks in the way of the gospel) do come.[182]

In the meantime, in the midst of these troubles, it's a great and sweet refreshment to wait and hope for an escape to

---

[181] Casaubon writes that: "[There is] an objection against Christianity, the most considerable in point of credibility that ever was made or can be made, and which has kept more people from embracing the Christian faith than any other thing that I know, of which many examples might be given from history. The question is . . . how it could be that . . . the great Lord and Governor of the world could be contained in the womb of a virgin . . . [so that a scoffer might] deride Christianity by talking of the virgin Mary and her Baby God. . . . If it be said the matter might easily be resolved by distinguishing of two natures in one Person, that indeed may easily be said, however this conjunction or union of God (the God of all Eternity) and man born of a virgin at such a time etc. may not so easily be believed or made credible . . . the more we apprehend God's greatness and omnipotence, which makes other miracles probable, the more this makes, or seems to make this union the more improbable and incredible . . . An incredible thing, if it suggests omnipotence, may be believed of God. The creation of the world from nothing . . . clearly suggests omnipotence. But if we say that God has assumed (or, clothed himself with) a body; that is to unclothe him of his divinity . . . to make him no god." Casaubon, *Of Credulity*, 120–23, modernized.

[182] "If any of you put a stumbling block before one of these little ones who believe in me, it would be better for you if a great millstone were fastened around your neck and you were drowned in the depth of the sea. Woe to the world because of stumbling blocks! Occasions for stumbling are bound to come, but woe to the one by whom the stumbling block comes!" Matthew 18:6–7.

CHAPTER 3: ANSWERING OBJECTIONS

mount Moriah,[183] the land of vision above where all these shades of gloomy night shall vanish away and an eternal day of clear light and peace shall shine on them "who love our Lord Jesus in sincerity,"[184] in whose glorious dignity I rejoice. Furthermore, I desire to boast and glory in this exalted and enthroned redeemer, for "worthy is the Lamb to receive glory, and honor, and blessing, and power."[185] Amen! So be it!

Now to him who loved us and washed us from our sins in his own blood, and has made us kings and priests to God, even the Father, to him be glory and dominion forever.[186] But this I confess to you, that according to the way, which they call "heresy," I worship the God of my fathers, believing all things which are written in the law and the prophets.[187]

---

[183] The mountain on which Solomon built the first Temple (2 Chronicles 3:1).
[184] Ephesians 6:24.
[185] Revelation 5:12.
[186] Revelation 1:5–6.
[187] Acts 24:14.

BIBLIOGRAPHY

Adams, Marilyn McCord. *What Sort of Human Nature? Medieval Philosophy and the Systematics of Christology*. Milwaukee: Marquette University Press, 1999.

Alexander, Caleb. *An Essay on the Real Deity of Jesus Christ*. Boston, 1791.

Aquinas, Thomas. *Summa Theologica,* Vol. 2. Translated by Fathers of the English Dominican Province and Daniel J. Sullivan. Chicago: Encyclopedia Britannica, 1952 [1273].

Augustine of Hippo. *Answer to Maximinus the Arian*. In *Arianism and Other Heresies*, translated by Roland J. Teske. Hyde Park: New City Press, 1995 [c. 428 CE].

Baxter, Richard. *A Paraphrase on the New Testament, with Notes Doctrinal and Practical.* 2nd ed. London, 1695 [1685].

Boyse, Joseph. *The Difference between Mr. E— [Emlyn] and the Protestant Dissenting Ministers of D— [Dublin] Truly Represented*. Dublin, 1702.

———. *A Vindication of the True Deity of Our Blessed Saviour: In Answer to a Pamphlet, Entitled, An Humble Enquiry Into the Scripture-Account of Jesus Christ*. London, 1704.

Calamy, Edmund. *Thirteen Sermons concerning the Doctrine of the Trinity*. London, 1722.

Casaubon, Meric. *Of Credulity and Incredulity in Things Divine and Spiritual: Wherein, (Among other Things) A True and Faithful Account is Given of the Platonick Philosophy, As it hath Reference to Christianity: As also the Business of Witches and Witchcraft, Against a Late Writer, Fully Argued and Disputed.* London, 1670.

Cicero, Marcus Tullius. *The Nature of the Gods*. Translated by P.G. Walsh. New York: Oxford University Press, 1998 [45–44 BCE].

Clarke, Samuel. *The Scripture-Doctrine of the Trinity, Wherein Every Text in the New Testament relating to That Doctrine is Distinctly Considered; and the Divinity of Our Blessed Saviour, according to the Scriptures, Proved and Explained.* In *The Works of Samuel Clarke, D. D., Late Rector of St. James's Westminster; in Four Volumes.*, Vol. 4., edited by J. Clarke. London, 1738 [1712].

Colligan, J.H. *The Arian Movement in England*. Manchester: Publications of the University of Manchester, 1913.

Cross, Richard. *Communicatio Idiomatum: Reformation Christological Debates*. New York: Oxford University Press, 2019.

BIBLIOGRAPHY

Dixon, Philip. *Nice and Hot Disputes: The Doctrine of the Trinity in the Seventeenth Century.* New York: T&T Clark, 2003.

Drummond, William Hamilton. *An Explanation and Defence of the Principles of Protestant Dissent.* London, 1842.

Emlyn, Sollom. "Memoirs of the Life and Writings of Mr. Thomas Emlyn." In *The Works of Mr. Thomas Emlyn.* 4th ed. Volume 1. London, 1746.

Emlyn, Thomas. *An Answer to Dr. Waterland on the Head of Worship Paid to Jesus Christ.* In *The Works of Mr. Thomas Emlyn.* 4th ed. Volume 1. London, 1746 [1706].

———. *The Case of Mr. E. [Emlyn] in relation to the Difference between Him and Some Dissenting Ministers of the City of D. [Dublin] which He Supposes is Greatly Mis-understood.* In *The Works of Mr. Thomas Emlyn.* 4th ed. Volume 1. London, 1746. [1702].

———. *Extracts from An Humble Inquiry into the Scripture-Account of Jesus Christ.* Boston, 1790 [1702].

———. *An Humble Inquiry into the Scripture-Account of Jesus Christ: Or, A Short Argument concerning His Deity and Glory, according to the Gospel.* In *The Works of Mr. Thomas Emlyn.* 4th ed. Volume 1. London, 1746 [1702].

———. *An Humble Inquiry into the Scripture-Account of Jesus Christ: Or, A Short Argument concerning His Deity and Glory, according to the Gospel.* 5th ed. Boston, 1756 [1702].

———. *Remarks on Mr. Charles Leslie's First Dialogue on the Socinian Controversy*. London, 1706.

———. "A True Narrative of the Proceedings of the Dissenting Ministers of Dublin against Mr. Thomas Emlyn." In *The Works of Mr. Thomas Emlyn*. 4th ed. Volume 1. London, 1746 [1719].

———. *A Vindication of the Worship of the Lord Jesus Christ, on Unitarian Principles. In Answer to What is Said on that Head, by Mr. Joseph Boyse, in His Vindication of the Deity of Jesus Christ*. In *The Works of Mr. Thomas Emlyn*. 4th ed. Volume 1. London, 1746 [1706].

———. *The Works of Mr. Thomas Emlyn*. 4th ed. Volume 1. Edited by Sollom Emlyn. London, 1746. Reprint: lulu.com, 2010.

Eusebius of Caesarea. *Against Marcellus*. In *Eusebius of Caesarea: Against Marcellus and On Ecclesiastical Theology*, translated by Kelley McCarthy Spoerl and Markus Vinzent. Washington, DC: Catholic University of America Press, 2017 [336 CE].

———. *On Ecclesiastical Theology*. In *Eusebius of Caesarea: Against Marcellus and On Ecclesiastical Theology*, translated by Kelley McCarthy Spoerl and Markus Vinzent. Washington, DC: Catholic University of America Press, 2017 [c. 337–39 CE].

The Future State: Or, A Discourse Attempting Some Display of the Soul's Happiness. In regard to that Eternally Progressive Knowledge, Or Eternal Increase of Knowledge and the Consequences of it which is Amongst the Blessed in Heaven. London, 1683.

BIBLIOGRAPHY

Gaston, Thomas E. *Dynamic Monarchianism: The Earliest Christology?* White House: Theophilus Press, 2021.

Gibson, William. "The Persecution of Thomas Emlyn (1703–1705)." *Journal of Church and State* 48, no. 3 (Summer 2006): 525–39.

Goodwin, Thomas. *The Heart of Christ in Heaven, Towards Sinners on Earth: Or, A Treatise Demonstrating the Gracious Disposition and Tender Affection of Christ, in His Human Nature Now in Glory, unto His Members, Under All Sorts of Infirmities, Either of Sin or Misery.* In his *Christ Set Forth.* London, 1831 [1645].

Gregory I, Pope. "Letter of Pope Gregory I to Eulogius, Patriarch of Alexandria. August, 600 A.D." In *The Faith of the Early Fathers*, Vol. 3. Edited and translated by William A. Jurgens. Collegeville: The Liturgical Press, 1979 [600 CE].

Grillmeier, Aloys and Theresia Hainthaler. *Christ in Christian Tradition, Volume II: From the Council of Chalcedon (451) to Gregory the Great (590–604).* Translated by John Cawte and Pauline Allen. Louisville: Westminster John Knox Press, 1995.

Hanson, R.P.C. *The Search for the Christian Doctrine of God: The Arian Controversy 318–381.* Edinburgh: T&T Clark, 1988.

Harris, Murray. *Jesus as God: The New Testament Use of* Theos *in Reference to Jesus.* Eugene: Wipf and Stock, 1992.

Hasker, William. "Objections to Social Trinitarianism." *Religious Studies* 46, no. 4 (2010): 421–39.

Howe, John. *A Calm and Sober Enquiry concerning the Possibility of a Trinity in the Godhead*. London, 1694.

Howell, T.B., ed. *A Complete Collection of State Trials and Proceedings for High Treason and Other Crimes and Misdemeanors from the Earliest Period to the Year 1783*, Vol. 2. London, 1816.

Hyndman, R. J. "Biblical Monotheism Today." In *One God, the Father: A Compendium of Essays*. Edited by Thomas E. Gaston. London: Willow Publications, 2013.

Innocent XI. *A Decree Made at Rome, the Second of March, 1679, Condemning Some Opinions of the Jesuits and Other Casuists*. Translated by G. Burnet. London, 1679.

Irenaeus of Lyons. *Against Heresies [a.k.a. A Refutation and Overthrow of Knowledge Falsely So-Called]*. In *The Ante-Nicene Fathers: Volume 1 – The Apostolic Fathers with Justin and Irenaeus*. Edited and translated by Alexander Roberts, James Donaldson, and Arthur Cleveland Coxe. Edinburgh, 1885 [c. 175–89]. Reprint, New York: Cosimo, 2007.

Irons, Charles Lee and Danny Andre Dixon and Dustin R. Smith. *The Son of God: Three Views on the Identity of Jesus*. Eugene: Wipf & Stock, 2015.

Justin Martyr, *Dialogue with Trypho*. In *St. Justin Martyr: Dialogue with Trypho*. Translated by Thomas Wells, revised by Thomas Halton, edited by Michael Slusser. Washington, DC: The Catholic University of America Press, 2003 [c. 155–61].

Lamson, Alvan. *The Church of the First Three Centuries: Or, Notices of the Lives and Opinions of Some of the Early Fathers, with Special Reference to the Doctrine of the Trinity, Illustrating its Late Origin and Gradual Formation*. Edited by Ezra Abbot and Henry Ierson. London: British and Foreign Unitarian Association, 1875 [1860]. Reprint, Toronto: University of Toronto Libraries, 2012.

le Comte, Louis. *Memoirs and Observations Topographical, Physical, Mathematical, Mechanical, Natural, Civil, and Ecclesiastical. Made in a Late Journey through the Empire of China and Published in Several Letters*. 3rd ed. London, 1699 [1696].

Leftow, Brian. "Anti-Social Trinitarianism." In *The Trinity: An Interdisciplinary Symposium on the Trinity*. Edited by S. T. Davis, D. Kendall and G. O'Collins. New York: Oxford University Press, 1999.

Leslie, Charles. *The Rehearsal* 2, no. 29. London, 1706.

Limborch, Philip van. *Institutiones Theologiae Christianae, ad Praxin Pietatis et Promotionem Pacis, Christianae Unice Directae*. Amsterdam, 1686. English translation: *A Compleat System or Body of Divinity, both Speculative and Practical, Founded on Scripture and Reason*. Translated by William Jones. London, 1702.

Locke, John. "A Letter Concerning Toleration." In *Locke on Toleration*. Edited by Richard Vernon. Cambridge: Cambridge University Press, 2010.

BIBLIOGRAPHY

Loyola, Ignatius. *The Spiritual Exercises of St. Ignatius: A New Translation Based on Studies in the Language of the Autograph.* Translated by Louis J. Puhl. Westminster: Newman Press, 1951 [1548].

Makower, Felix. *The Constitutional History and Constitution of the Church of England.* London, 1895.

Matthews, George. *An Account of the Trial, on 14th June, 1703, Before the Court of Queen's Bench, Dublin, of the Reverend Thomas Emlyn for a Publication Against the Doctrine of the Trinity, with a Sketch of His Associations, Predecessors, and Successors.* Belfast, 1839.

Mist, Nathaniel. *A Collection of Miscellany Letters, selected out of Mist's Weekly Journal,* Vol. 2. London: 1722–27.

Mott, Frederick B. "Growth of Unitarian Thought Since the Protestant Reformation." In *The Unitarian,* Vol. 4. Edited by J.T. Sunderland. Boston, 1889.

Newton, Isaac. *Optice: Sive De Reflexionibus, Refractionibus, Inflexionibus & Coloribus Lucis. Libri Tres.* [*Optics: Or, On the Reflections, Refractions, Inflections, and Colors of Light. In Three Books.*] London, 1706.

Nye, Stephen. *A Brief History of the Unitarians, Called also Socinians. In Four Letters, Written to a Friend.* London, 1687.

———. *A Discourse concerning Nominal and Real Trinitarians.* London, 1695.

———. *The Doctrine of the Holy Trinity, and the Manner of Our Saviour's Divinity; As They Are Held in the Catholic Church, and the Church of England.* London, 1701.

———. *The Grounds and Occasions of the Controversy concerning the Unity of God, &c, the Methods by which It Has Been Managed, and the Means to Compose it.* London, 1698.

———. *Institutions, concerning the Holy Trinity, And the Manner of Our Saviour's Divinity.* London, 1703.

———. *Observations on the Four Letters of Dr. John Wallis concerning the Trinity and the Creed of Athanasius.* London, 1691.

———. *A Resolution of the Objections against the Doctrine of the Holy Trinity: Together with the Church-Terms of Communion relating to that Doctrine* in *Two Treatises concerning the Trinity and the Divinity of Our Blessed Saviour.* London, 1703.

———. *A Sober Expostulation with the Gentleman and Citizens of Mr. Emlin's* [sic] *Juries in Dublin, concerning Their* Billa Vera *and Verdict, June 14, 1703.* n.d.

Origen. *Commentary on the Gospel According to John Books 1–10.* Translated by Ronald E. Heine. Washington, DC: The Catholic University of America Press, 1989 [c. 248 CE].

———. *Origen: Contra Celsum* [*Against Celsus*]. Translated by Henry Chadwick. New York: Cambridge University Press, 1953 [c. 246–48 CE].

———. *Origen: On First Principles*, Vol. 1. Edited and translated by John Behr. New York: Oxford University Press, 2017 [c. 229–30 CE].

Pfizenmaier, Thomas C. *The Trinitarian Theology of Dr. Samuel Clarke (1675–1729): Context, Sources, and Controversy*. Leiden: Brill, 1997.

Philo of Alexandria. *The Decalogue*. In *The Works of Philo, New Updated Ed*. Translated by C.D. Yonge. Hendrickson, 1993 [c. 30–40 CE].

———. *The Special Laws I*. In *The Works of Philo, New Updated Ed.*, translated by C.D. Yonge. Hendrickson, 1993 [c. 30–40 CE].

Schoenheit, John, Mark H. Graeser, and John A. Lynn. *One God and One Lord: Reconsidering the Cornerstone of the Christian Faith*. 4th ed. Indianapolis: Spirit & Truth Fellowship International, 2010.

Sherlock, William. *A Vindication of the Doctrine of the Trinity and of the Incarnation of the Son of God: Occasioned by the Brief Notes on the Creed of St. Athanasius, and the Brief History of the Unitarians or Socinians*. London, 1690.

South, Robert. *Animadversions upon Dr. Sherlock's Book, Entitled a Vindication of the Holy and Ever Blessed Trinity*. London, 1693.

Sparks, Jared. *A Collection of Essays and Tracts in Theology, From Various Authors with Biographical and Critical Notes,* Vol. 4. Boston, 1824.

Steele, Richard [Benjamin Hoadly]. *Account of the State of the Roman Catholic Religion Throughout the World.* London, 1715.

Stillingfleet, Edward. *Fifty Sermons Preached Upon Several Occasions.* London, 1707.

"Textus Receptus [of the Apostles' Creed]." In *Creeds of the Churches.* 3rd ed. Edited by John H. Leith. Atlanta: John Knox Press, 1982 [c. 700].

Thomas, Roger. "The Non-Subscription Controversy amongst Dissenters in 1719: The Salters' Hall Debate." *The Journal of Ecclesiastical History* 4, no. 2 (1953): 162–86.

Tillotson, John. "Sermon 54—Concerning the Divinity of our Blessed Saviour. Preached in the Church of St. Lawrence-Jewry, Jan. 6, 1679." In *The Works of Dr. John Tillotson, Late Archbishop of Canterbury.* Edited by Thomas Birch. London, 1820 [1679].

Trowell, Stephen. "Unitarian and/or Anglican: The Relationship of Unitarianism to the Church from 1687 to 1698," *Bulletin of the John Rylands Library* 78 (1996): 77–101.

Tuggy, Dale. "Clarifying Catholic Christologies." 21st Century Reformation, July 31, 2017. YouTube video, 59:51, https://youtu.be/s6wK-lRZP-k.

———. "Jesus's argument in John 10," *trinities* (blog). November 14, 2014. https://trinities.org/blog/jesuss-argument-in-john-10/.

———. "The Lost Early History of Unitarian Christian Theology," 21st Century Reformation, September 30, 2013. YouTube video, 43:51, https://youtu.be/oHnlw4iMhE8.

———. "podcast 165 – Alvan Lamson's On the Doctrine of Two Natures in Jesus Christ – Part 1," December 26, 2016, *trinities*, Podcast, 40:35, https://trinities.org/blog/podcast-165-alvan-lamsons-on-the-doctrine-of-two-natures-in-jesus-christ-part-1/.

———. "podcast 166 – Alvan Lamson's On the Doctrine of Two Natures in Jesus Christ – Part 2," January 3, 2017, *trinities*, Podcast, 33:31, https://trinities.org/blog/podcast-166-alvan-lamsons-on-the-doctrine-of-two-natures-in-jesus-christ-part-2/.

———. "Trinity." *The Stanford Encyclopedia of Philosophy* (Winter 2020 Edition). Edited by Edward N. Zalta, https://plato.stanford.edu/archives/win2020/entries/trinity/.

Tuggy, Dale and Chris Date. *Is Jesus Human and Not Divine?* Apollo: Aeropagus, 2020.

Van Den Berg, Johannes. *Religious Currents and Cross-Currents: Essays on Early Modern Protestantism and the Protestant Enlightenment.* Leiden: Brill, 1999.

Van Doren, Charles. *The Joy of Reading.* Naperville: Sourcebooks, 2008.

BIBLIOGRAPHY

Wallace, Daniel. "The Textual Problem in 1 John 5:7-8," Bible.org, 1998. https://bible.org/article/textual-problem-1-john-578.

Wallace, Robert. *Antitrinitarian Biography, or Sketches of the Lives and Writings of Distinguished Antitrinitarians,* Vol. 3. London, 1850.

Wallis, John. *The Doctrine of the Blessed Trinity, Briefly Explained in a Letter to a Friend.* London: T. Parkhurst, 1690.

Whiston, William. *Memoirs of the Life and Writings of Mr. William Whiston,* Part 2. London, 1749.

———. *The True Origin of the Sabellian and Athanasian Doctrines of the Trinity.* London, 1720.

Whitby, Daniel. *A Paraphrase and Commentary on the New Testament.* Vol. 2. London, 1703.

———. *Hysterai phrontides: Or The Last Thoughts of Dr. Whitby.* Edited by Arthur Ashley Sykes. London, 1841 [1727]. Reprint, *The Last Thoughts of Dr. Whitby*, lulu.com, 2007.

Wilbur, Earl Morse. *A History of Unitarianism: In Transylvania, England, and America.* Boston: Beacon Press, 1945.

Williams, Rowan. *Arius: Heresy and Tradition.* Grand Rapids: Eerdmans, 2002 [1987].

APPENDIX A:

The Complete Bibliography of Thomas Emlyn

"How We May Walke in the Feare of God." January 17th, 1689.

"How We May Redeem Time." January 24th, 1689.

The Suppression of Public Vice, an Honourable Employment. Dublin, 1698.

Funeral Consolations, A Discourse from John XIV. Ver. 28, Being the First Sermon He Preached After the Death of his Wife, Mrs. Esther Emlyn, Who Died October 13th, 1701. Written 1701, first published in Dublin, 1703.

The Case of Mr. E in relation to the Difference Between Him and Some Dissenting Ministers of the City of Dublin. London, 1702; Dublin, 1703.

An Humble Inquiry into the Scripture-Account of Jesus Christ: A Short Argument concerning His Deity and Glory, according to the Gospel. Dublin, 1702.

"Letter to William Manning, Dec. 23rd, 1703." *Monthly Repository* 20, no. 240 (December 1825): 705-9.

APPENDIX A

General Remarks on Mr. Boyse's Vindication of the True Deity of Our Blessed Saviour. Written 1704, first published in *Works,* Vol. I. 1746.

"Letter to William Manning, April 8th, 1704." *Monthly Repository* 21, no. 242 (February 1826): 87-89.

"Meditations on My Afflicted Condition." 1704.

"Letter to William Manning, March 21st, 1705." *Monthly Repository* 21, no. 244 (April 1826): 203-4.

"Letter to William Manning, June 8th, 1706." *Monthly Repository* 21, no. 246 (June 1826): 333-34.

A Vindication of the Worship of the Lord Jesus Christ, on Unitarian Principles, in Answer to Mr. J. Boyse. London, 1706.

"A Letter to Dr. Willis (Now Bishop of Winchester) Occasioned by his Sermon before the House of Commons. Nov. 5th, 1705." Written 1705, first printed London, 1719.

A Brief Vindication of the Bishop of Glocester's Discourse concerning the Descent of the Man Christ Jesus from Heaven. London, 1706.

The Supreme Deity of God the Father Demonstrated, Being a Short, but Full Answer to Dr. Sherlock's Proofs of Our Saviour's Divinity, or Whatever Can Be Urged Against the Supremacy of the First Person of the Holy Trinity. London, 1706.

An Examination of Mr. Leslie's Last Dialogue, relating to the Satisfaction of Jesus Christ, Together with Some Remarks on Dr. Stillingfleet's True Reasons of Christ's Sufferings. London, 1708.

Remarks on Mr. Charles Leslie's First Dialogue on the Socinian Controversy. London, 1708.

A Vindication of the Said Remarks. London, 1708.

APPENDIX A

Mr. Wall's History of Infant-Baptism Improved, or a Just Occasion Taken from Thence to Inquire, Whether There Be Any Necessity (Upon His Principles) for the Continual Use of Baptism Among the Posterity of Baptized Christians. London, 1709.

"Letter to William Manning, Oct. 10th, 1710." *Monthly Repository* 12, no. 239 (July 1817): 388.

"Letter to William Manning, Dec. 5th, 1710." *Monthly Repository* 12, no. 239 (July 1817): 388-89.

"Some Observations on the Representation by the Lower House of Convocation to Queen Anne." June, 1711.

The Previous Question to the Several Questions About Valid and Invalid Baptism. London, 1712.

A Full Inquiry into the Original Authority of that Text, 1 John v. 7, There Are Three that Bear Record in Heaven, Containing an Account of Dr. Mill's Evidences from Antiquity, For and Against Its Being Genuine, with an Examination of His Judgement thereupon. Humbly Addressed to Both House of Convocation now Assembled. London, 1715.

Dr. Bennet's New Theory of the Trinity Examined, or, Some Considerations on His Discourse of the Ever-Blessed Trinity in Unity, and His Examination of Dr. Clarke's Scripture-Doctrine of the Trinity. London, 1718.

An Answer to Mr. Martin's Critical Dissertation on 1 John 5.7, There are Three that Bear Record, etc., Shewing the Insufficiency of his Proofs and the Errors of his Suppositions by which he Attempts to Establish the Authority of that Text from Supposed Manuscripts. London, 1719.

APPENDIX A

Remarks on a Book, Entitled, The Doctrine of the Blessed Trinity Stated and Defended, by Four London Ministers, with an Appendix concerning the Equality of the Three Persons, and Mr. Jurieu's Testimony to the Primitive Doctrine in this Point. London, 1719.

The Revd. Mr. Trosse's Arguments Answered, relating to the Lord Jesus Christ, and the Deity of the Holy Ghost, taken from His Catechism, and Sermon on Luke 22:31. London, 1719.

A True Narrative of the Proceedings of the Dissenting Ministers of Dublin against Mr. Thomas Emlyn; and of His Prosecution (at Some of the Dissenters Instigation) in the Secular Court, and His Sufferings thereupon, for His Humble Inquiry into the Scripture-Account of the Lord Jesus Christ. London, 1719.

A Reply to Mr. Martin's Examination of the Answer to His Dissertation on 1 John 5.7. London, 1720.

Observations on Dr. Waterland's Notions in relation to Polytheism, Ditheism, the Son's Consubstantiality with, and Inferiority to the Father. Written 1731, first published in *Works*, Vol. 2. 1746.

A Collection of Tracts Stating Some Important Points relating to the Deity, Worship, and Satisfaction of the Lord Jesus Christ. London, 1731.

"To My Dear Grandson Thomas Emlyn." 1739.

Sermons. London, 1742.

"Memoirs of the Life and Sentiments of the Reverend Dr. Samuel Clarke." Written 1731, first published in *Works*, Vol. 2. 1746.

"Animadversions on Dr. Edmund Calamy's Allegation of Justin Martyr's Testimony concerning the Trinity." n.d.

"Concerning Episcopacy, I Take it to be Thus." n.d.

APPENDIX A

"Of Apparent Contradictions, and the Use of Reason in Religion." n.d.

"Of Church Discipline." n.d.

"Of the Law to Adam." n.d.

"Of the Magistrate's Authority in the Church." n.d.

"Of a Mediator." n.d.

SCRIPTURE INDEX

Genesis
1   106

Exodus
4:16   36
7:1   36
22:28   36

Numbers
12:7   80

Deuteronomy
10:17   37

Joshua
22:22   37

Judges
9:1-21   79

2 Samuel
14:20   70

1 Kings
8:39   72, 75

2 Kings
6:8-12   75

1 Chronicles
29:20   91

2 Chronicles
3:1   111

Psalms
8:5   36
8:6   43
50:1   37
82:1   36
97:7   36
97:9   89
86:8   38
110:1-2   45
135:5   38, 89
136:1-2   89
147:5   56

Isaiah
40:15   71
40:25   103-4
41:23   56

SCRIPTURE INDEX

46:9-10	75

Jeremiah

17:5	86
17:10	72

Malachi

1:14	91
4:2	78

Matthew

9:9	72-89
10:16	61
18:6-7	110
19:17	53-55
24:3	60
24:36	56-67, 69
27:46	40
28:19	63
28:18-20	45, 79, 87, 90

Mark

2:8	75
10:17	55
10:18	53-55
13:32	56-67, 69, 83, 84
14:22-25	98, 101

Luke

2:52	83
6:8	75
7:39	70
18:19	53-55
22:69	73

John

2:19-22	67
2:25	72-89
4:19	70
4:29	70
5:19-20	43, 52
5:22-23	78, 90
5:26-27	43, 52, 78, 88
5:30	42, 43, 51, 52
5:43	42
6:6	55
6:38	42
6:53-55	98
7:17	40
8:42	40-41
10:28-29	42, 108
10:30	107
10:34-36	36, 47
11:11-13	67
11:34	83
14:9-10	53, 107
14:28	42, 103
16:30	69, 71
17:3	37
20:17	40, 69
21:23	55

Acts

1:7	71
1:9-11	73
2:22	96, 106
2:33	73
2:36-37	48, 96
2:41	97
5:1-11	75
5:31	48, 73

SCRIPTURE INDEX

8:14	100
10:34-38	97
15:18	56
17:31	88
24:14	111

Romans
8:38-39	108
9:5	44
11:35	52
16:27	74

1 Corinthians
1:23	106
8:5	39
8:4-6	41
8:6	34, 41
11:3	43, 103
12:10	75
12:12-31	81
15:24-29	43-44, 79-80

2 Corinthians
4:4	36, 100

Ephesians
1:3	38
1:17	38, 43
1:20	73
1:21	38
1:22	45, 78
4:5-6	41
4:15-16	85
6:24	111

Philippians
2:6	49
2:8-11	43, 73, 90-91

Colossians
1:15	37, 100
1:16	107
1:26-27	73
2:9	80, 106-7

1 Timothy
1:17	74
2:5	91-94
3:16	73
6:16	74

2 Timothy
1:12	108

Hebrews
1-2	107
1:1-4	73, 106-7
1:8-9	48
2:8	45
2:14-18	87
3:1-2, 5-6	80
4:15-16a	81

1 Peter
2:21-24	60-61
3:22	73

1 John
2:20	70
5:7	107

SCRIPTURE INDEX

Revelation

1:1-2	76
1:5-6	38, 111
1:14	88
1:18	107
2-3	76
2:23	72-89
5:6	85, 87
5:12	73, 111
15:4	74
17:14	38
19:12	88

Manufactured by Amazon.ca
Acheson, AB

13069089R00081